QUIPS, QUOTES, & QUICK STARTERS

*Great for Lessons and Discussions in
Classroom Guidance, Small Group,
& Individual Counseling*

Grades 5-12

By Tom Carr, M.S.

youth light
inc.

© 2007 by YouthLight, Inc.
Chapin, SC 29036

Cover Design and Layout by Diane Florence
Project Editing by Susan Bowman

ISBN: 9781598500172

Library of Congress Number
2007920027

10 9 8 7 6 5 4 3 2 1
Printed in the United States

TABLE OF CONTENTS

INTRODUCTION

Seed before seek

Several months ago I started on my journey to write this "motivational" book. I became intrigued with the idea of adults planting seeds in young people as a way to inspire them on their travels to achieving personal goals. I opened my edition of *Webster's Dictionary* to find the description of the word 'seed.' As I read about the word 'seed,' I noticed that the very next word in the dictionary was 'seek.' I paused for a moment and thought, "That's it! In the dictionary, seed comes before seek. We need to provide all young people with a seed before they can become motivated to seek their goals, dreams and aspirations." This book is my attempt to help teachers, counselors, parents, youth group leaders, clergy, and other caring adults plant seeds in today's youth.

We can become "World Changers"

The more seeds we plant, the more we can change the world. We may not see the immediate, positive results of our plantings, but future generations may reap the benefits of our work. Consider the following examples of planting seeds today in order to help people in the future.

■ Author Ophia D. Smith tells us, "The people of Old Spain had a maxim that whoever eats a fruit must plant a seed; otherwise, he is ungrateful to the past and unjust to the coming generation. Whenever a Spaniard ate a fruit, he dug a hole in the ground with his toe, placed the seed therein, and scraped a bit of earth over it with his foot. As a consequence, there was an abundance of fruit in Spain to be had for the taking, along highways and in remote places."

Think of the adults in your life when you were a child who planted seeds in you. What did they say or do that inspired you? Others planted seeds in you, now it's time for you to do some planting!

■ Loren Eiseley is a well-known and respected nature writer. He spent many years hiking throughout the United States. He often thought of himself as a world changer because he always carried seeds with him. In his book, *The Lost Notebooks of Loren Eiseley*, he wrote, "When I climb I almost always carry seeds with me in my pocket.....I have carried seeds up the sheer walls of mesas.....I have dropped sunflower seeds on stony mesa tops and planted cactus in Alpine meadows amidst bluebells and the sound of water. I have sowed northern seeds south and southern seeds north and crammed acorns into the most unlikely places. You can call it a hobby if you like. In a small way I am a world changer and leaving my mark on the future."

Could it be that a certain beautiful flower growing on a mountain side is there because of people like Eiseley? Are you a world changer? Are you planting seeds today in our children that will make you a world changer; then, will these children eventually become world changers themselves?

■ During World War I thousands of soldiers spent years living in mud, dirt, and trenches in Germany and France. Their world was drab, dark, colorless, and barren. Because of the bombing, they would go months without seeing a tree, green grass, or a flower. Whenever the soldiers wrote home, they asked their friends and families to send them seeds. In the book, *Defiant Gardens*, author Kenneth L. Helphand gives an example of how important seeds were to the soldiers. He writes, "When the countryside yielded little, soldiers pursued other avenues to satisfy their longing. German soldier Wily Holscher wrote from the trenches in Champagne in 1916, 'Would you be so kind as to send me some

4

flower seeds? There is nothing very nice to look at about my billet, and, so I don't know how long I may be stuck here, I want to grow some flowers. Please send me sweet-peas, convolvulus, sunflower, flax, mignonette, etc. I want to cover the unsightly earth with verdure."

Even though some of these soldiers knew they might be killed or transferred, they still had a desire to plant seeds and they were willing to be patient waiting for them to grow. The flowers, fruits, and vegetables gave them something to look forward to in their dark, dirty environment. Their eyes were on the future. It's been said millions of times, "The children are our future." Are you planting seeds for the future?

■ We all know the legend of Johnny Appleseed. His real name was John Chapman. On his travels he planted apple seeds, knowing that he may not be alive when the trees produced fruit. He planted for the future. Chapman also planted flower seeds and medicinal plants, such as fennel, to help the settlers.

■ There is an old Sufi tale called, "The Vine." A certain man planted a vine, known as being of a kind which produces eatable grapes only after thirty years. It so happened that as he was planting it, the Commander of the Faithful passed by, paused and said, "You are a remarkable optimist if you hope to live until that vine bears fruit." The man responded, "Perhaps I shall not, but at least my successors will live to benefit from my work, as we all profit from the work of our predecessors."

We need to be as optimistic as this man. Again, we may not see immediate results from the planting of seeds in our children, but people in the future will be glad we did.

Where to get your seeds

I hope you agree with me on the importance of planting seeds, but you might wonder where to get these special seeds. I suggest you get them out of your **Q Garden**. What is the Q Garden you ask? Think of this book as the garden. It contains hundreds of Q's. As you travel through the book (garden) you'll see rows of Quips, Quotes, and Quick Starters. Every day on your way to school or other settings in which you work with young people, stop by the garden and pick a Q (seed) and take it with you.

If you need a light-hearted, clever, witty, or thought-provoking message to share with your students, pick a **Quip**. Quips are great seeds to start the day off on a good note. If you need a more serious message, pick a **Quote**. Quotes are categorized into 18 different topics. So, if you are concerned about, let's say 'honesty,' then read an honesty quote to your children. Following each quote is a set of questions to "prime the pump" and jump-start some good classroom discussions. In the back of this book you'll find a section called, "They Said It," which gives a brief biography of each "quoter." Some days you may want to pick a **Quick Starter** from your Q Garden. Quick Starters are short (true) stories that you can read to the children, or they can read on their own. Follow up with a discussion.

Final notes

This book can be used in classes, upper elementary through high school. A small number of Q's may be inappropriate for younger children, use good judgment. Q's can also be very effective with individuals and small groups. So, head to the garden, pick some Q's (seeds) and share them with the children. Remember, seed comes before seek.

Academics & Education
QUIPS

■ Privacy please!

Do you need peace and quiet while doing homework? The writer Jack London did. When he needed privacy he had this sign posted outside his door:

#1. Please do not enter without knocking.
#2. Please do not knock.

■ The first Nerd on record

The first nerd on record is the one in Dr. Seuss's 1950 book, *If I Ran the Zoo*:

And then, just to show them, I'll sail to
Ka-Troo
And bring back an It-Kutch, a Peep
and a Proo
A Nerkle, a Nerd, and a Seersucker,
too!

■ A voracious reader

Author, Eric Hoffer mysteriously went blind when he was only seven years of age. He unexpectedly regained his sight at age fifteen. He was so afraid that blindness would return that he became obsessed with reading. He continued to read one book after another.

■ Finish, even if you finish last

Question: What do you call the student who finishes last in his/her graduation class at medical school? Answer: Doctor.

■ You better know your fractions

Pennsylvania farmers in the nineteenth century weren't going to be tricked when oil was discovered on their land and business tycoons offered them a percentage of the profits in exchange for drilling rights. Some farmers rejected the oil company's offer of 1/2 the profits and held out for 1/4 because 4 was larger than 2.

■ You're never too old to learn

After slavery was abolished in the 1860's many former slaves were hungry to learn to read. There was a 108-year-old lady who was determined to read the Bible before dying.

7

Academics & Education QUIPS

■ No one can take it away

The famous blues singer, B.B. King, expressed his feelings on the importance of education in his quote, "The beautiful thing about learning is that no one can take it away from you."

■ 100 poems

A famous poet was asked what she did to prepare herself before writing one poem. She replied, "I read at least one hundred poems written by other poets."

■ Football knowledge

Fifth grader, Jonathon Schilke, was a big football fan and he knew all the rules. His football knowledge garnered him national attention as he challenged his state's education department on one of their end-of-year exam questions. Here was the question:

How many total yards did the Falcons football team gain in this series of plays? +3, -2, +3, -1, +6?
Most everyone would answer: +9 yards. But here was Jonathon's concern. He knew that football teams get only four plays to get ten yards in order to get a first down. According to the question, the Falcons gained only three yards in four plays. That means they didn't get a first down so they wouldn't have gotten the ball for a fifth play. The state promised to be more careful the next time.

■ Wasting paper at school

"Students today depend on paper too much. They don't know how to write on a slate without getting dust all over themselves. They can't clean a slate properly. What will they do when they run out of paper?"   – *Principal's Association, 1815.*

■ A stinker of a tongue twister

What would you do if your teacher told you that in order to pass English class you had to read this tongue twister three times, as fast as you could?

The skunk sat on a stump.
The stump thunk the skunk stunk.
And the skunk thunk the stump stunk.

Academics & Education QUIPS

▪ Here is an interesting thought

President Harry S. Truman said, "The 'C' students run the world."
What do you think he meant by that?

▪ Books versus magazines

Gandhi once said, "Live as if you were to die tomorrow. Learn as if you were to live forever." In his fascinating book, The *Colony*, author John Tayman tells of a young man who was dying of leprosy in 1925. Harada was a very intelligent man who graduated with honors from the University of Hawaii. As he was dying, one of his friends asked him about his reading habits. Harada replied, "I've stopped reading books. I only read magazines now. There isn't much point in trying to keep on learning."

▪ Politeness at school

Here were a few suggestions given to students on how to be polite in school in 1890. These words of encouragement come from Benjamin Comegys', *Primer of Ethics.*

● *Always salute your teacher distinctly when you enter the schoolroom.*

● *Treat your teachers always as you would like to be treated, and ought to be treated, if you were a teacher.*

● *If your teacher seems to be harsh or partial, do not take it for granted that he is so; possibly you are mistaken. Wait a while.*

● *If there are brighter scholars in the class than you, be proud of them, praise them; do not dislike them; try by all fair means to excel them.*

▪ Take a break

Pippi Longstocking warns us, "Too much learning breaks even the healthiest."

Q 9

Academics & Education
QUOTES

Academics & Education
QUOTES

"In the case of good books, the point is not how many of them you get through, but rather how many can get through to you."

-Mortimer Adler

☞**PRIMING THE PUMP:** Can you think of at least one book that really got to you, one you not only enjoyed but sparked your interest? What made that book so special to you? Have you ever been guilty of rushing through books that were required reading? How often do you read and approximately how many books do you read every month?

"Intelligence and character, that is the goal of true education."

-Martin Luther King, Jr.

☞**PRIMING THE PUMP:** Can an intelligent person be truly successful in life without good character traits? Explain. Intelligence and character; which of these two do you think is most important and explain your answer? Many schools have Character Education programs. What are your thoughts about having such programs in school?

"I always keep myself in a position of being a student."

-Jackie Joyner-Kersee

☞**PRIMING THE PUMP:** Once you graduate from school do you cease being a student? Explain your response. Think of two or three reasons why people should continue to learn, read, and study, no matter how old they get? Even though Olympian and track star, Jackie Joyner-Kersee was one of the greatest athletes ever; do you think she continued to learn new strategies for improving her speed and agility? What happens to people who stop learning?

Academics & Education
QUOTES

"I found that if a young person cheats in school he has a tendency to cheat if life. It starts a trend as his heart begins to harden and this becomes a terrible danger."
-Billy Graham

☞**PRIMING THE PUMP:** Is it true, if a person cheats in school will he cheat in other areas of his life? What do you think Billy Graham means by "his heart hardens?" If you were an employer looking to hire someone, would you hire someone who has a history of cheating? Why not? How do you feel when you see students cheating? Did you ever study hard for an exam and got a low score while another student cheated and got a higher score than you? How did you feel about it and what did you do?

"It is possible to have a brain and not a mind. A brain is inherited— a mind is developed."
-Feurestein

☞**PRIMING THE PUMP:** How does one 'develop' a brain? Besides schoolwork, what activities do you engage in that help develop your brain? What are your thoughts on those who appear to have great intelligence but never utilize it or build on it?

"I think education is power. I think that being able to communicate with people is power. One of my main goals on the planet is to encourage people to empower themselves."
-Oprah Winfrey

☞**PRIMING THE PUMP:** What do you think Oprah means by 'power?' If education is power, how will that power help one to be successful in life? Can you think of a reason why being able to communicate well with others is considered 'power?' Oprah encourages people to empower themselves. What do you do to empower yourself?

Q 12

Academics & Education
QUOTES

"More people need to start spending as much time in the library as they do on the basketball court. If they took the idea that they could escape poverty through education, I think it would make a more basic and long-lasting change in the way things happened."

-Kareem Abdul-Jabbar

☞**PRIMING THE PUMP:** Former NBA great, Kareem Abdul-Jabbar, believes that young people have a good chance of escaping poverty through education. What do you think he means by that? Can you think of a couple reasons why promising young athletes still need to pursue a good education? How do you balance the time you spend on your interests, such as sports, with your academic time?

"Our research finds that people who do well in school not only possess skills that can be measured on tests, they have self-discipline, which is twice as important as IQ in predicting achievement."

-Angela Duckworth
-Martin Seligman

☞**PRIMING THE PUMP:** How can self-discipline be twice as important as IQ (intelligence) in predicting achievement? Can someone be intelligent but not self-disciplined? What are some study habits that self-disciplined students have that other students may not have? How can you tell if a student is self-disciplined? How do you show your parents and teachers that you are self-disciplined?

Q

13

Academics & Education
QUOTES

"The best predictors of who will perform adequately in life include attendance, ability to stick to a task, motivation, social skills, and knowing how to prioritize and organize tasks."

-James Comer

☞**PRIMING THE PUMP:** Give yourself a grade of A,B,C,D on how well you are presently doing with each of Comer's seven predictors. Can you think of a few reasons why attendance is so important at school and on a job? How do you keep yourself organized? What are some ways you keep yourself motivated in school?

"Education is not the filling of a pail, but the lighting of a fire."
-William Butler Yeats

☞**PRIMING THE PUMP:** Can you think of a couple teachers that 'lit your fire," and got you excited? What are a few things that teachers do to make class interesting and relevant? Which subjects do you find interesting? Which subjects are difficult for you to get excited about?

Q

14

Academics & Education
QUICK STARTERS

- *Why the First Webster's Dictionaries were Small*
- *Wow! We've Got Desks!*
- *Summer Vacations are too Long*

WHY THE FIRST WEBSTER'S DICTIONARIES WERE SMALL

Historian, Carl Sagan, said, "Frederick Douglas, the famous African-American poet, taught that literacy is the path from slavery to freedom. There are many kinds of slavery and many kinds of freedom, but reading is still the path." When slavery was abolished, Frederick Douglas and other African American leaders worked hard to educate the freed slaves. They had to get books into the hands of these freed people who were so eager to learn to read and write.

According to researcher, Heather Andrea Williams, in her book, *Self-taught*, "The book that African-Americans used most frequently to decode written English was Noah Webster's *Elementary Spelling Book*, popularly called 'the blue-black speller.' In 1784 Webster printed the first edition of his 'dictionary/spelling book' and by 1818 it had sold over 5 million copies. Most dictionaries today are rather large, but Webster's first editions were very small, measuring only about six by five inches. Why were they so small? The main reason was so the slaves could hide them in their shirts or pockets. Don't forget, many slaves were severely punished if there were caught with books. Another reason for their smallness was to keep their light, easy to carry. Many of the freed slaves would carry them around when they were working in the fields. Heather Andrea Williams tells of one slave work carried his book while planting. At the end of each plowed row he would rest, take out his little book and study.

We can learn a lot from Noah Webster and the slaves. Maybe we all should carry a book with us wherever we go. When we get a small break, we can sit down and learn something new!

WOW! WE'VE GOT DESKS!

Many students today in the United States take things for granted as they enter the school building. They know they'll have a desk, books, paper, pencils, computers, nutritious lunch, heat or air conditioning, and qualified, caring teachers. Now, let's travel to Africa with author Deborah Ellis who wrote an "eye-opening" book, *Our Stories, Our Songs: African Children Talk about AIDS."* She tells of her travels throughout Africa where she interviewed hundreds of children who were orphaned; their parents died from AIDS. She discovered that all these children were determined to read and write, and school was the highlight of their lives. But the schools they went to were often shacks with little or no books and other supplies. Many of the schools didn't even have desks.

Ellis talked with two girls who were elated when they finally got desks. Here are their stories.

Mavis, age 15: *For a long time my village didn't have a school. Then everyone got together and built one. We made mounds for the bricks, gathering the mud and baked bricks. They were able to make desks for the grade seven class. This is the most serious class. Up until today the rest of us had to sit on rocks in the yard, or on the floor in the classroom. But, as of today, thanks to UNICEF, we all have desks!*

Mary, age 13: *I live with my grandmother and my mother. My father died last spring; I don't know why he died, except that he was sick. I am the second child in my family. I have two brothers and sisters. Science and math are my best subjects. I'd like to be a teacher when I grow up. I'm so happy to have a desk! All my life I have sat on the floor of the classroom, or on a rock in the schoolyard. It is uncomfortable, and it is hard to write that way, although my mind is smart and I still learn. I know I will be a better student now. Having a desk makes me feel important. Having a desk makes me feel that someone else thinks I'm important.*

SUMMER VACATIONS ARE TOO LONG!

Have you ever heard of students who complained that summer vacations and holidays breaks were too long? Well, years ago, students wanted to spend as much time as they could at school; they were hungry to learn all they could! They were saddened when school closed for Christmas break and summer vacation.

Probably one of the most eager groups of children who wanted to learn was the freed slaves who had been deprived of an education. They flocked to school with a great desire to read and write. In her remarkable book, *Self-Taught*, Heather Andrea Williams goes into great detail on the unique strategies freed slaves implemented in order to learn. She tells how Booker T. Washington thought school was like paradise. He said, "I had no schooling whatever while I was a slave, though I remember on several occasions I went as far as the school door with one of my young mistresses to carry her books. The picture of several dozen boys and girls in a schoolroom engaged in study made a deep impression upon me, and I had a feeling that to get into a schoolhouse and study in this way would be about the same as getting into paradise."

Heather Andrea Williams shares these "nuggets" on how eager many of the freed slaves were on schooling:

- When Frederick Douglas was sent on errands by his master, he would carry a book and bread, trading the bread for help in reading the book.

- One slave traded boxing and wrestling lessons for writing lessons.

- As a young boy, Richard Parker picked up old nails and traded them for marbles that he used to pay white boys for reading lessons.

- Excited students would line up outside the school doors two or three hours before they opened. Here is what one South Carolina teacher said about the early arrivers. "Although classes were scheduled to begin at nine o'clock, children began to arrive at half past six in the morning, before teachers had even finished their breakfast."

- Many students refused to leave school at closing time.

- Students complained about vacations being too long. One teacher noted that at the start of Christmas vacation one student asked for a shorter vacation. Another teacher, on the last day of school, had several students, in tears, beg her not to close. One of Miss Doud's teary-eyed students said, "You ought not to stop school, for we are just beginning to learn."

Adversity
QUIPS

Adversity QUIPS

■ From danger to opportunity

The Chinese write the word "crisis" with two characters. One means danger, and the other means opportunity. Together they spell crisis.

■ Overcoming rejection

The well known author, Trollope traveled to London to pick up a rejected manuscript from his publisher. Although somewhat disappointed, he got on the train for the long ride home. While sitting in his seat, he picked up his bulky, rejected manuscript, turned it over and started writing a new book.

■ What is your AQ?

In his book, *The Adversity Quotient*, Paul Stoltz asks his readers, "When you face adversity, are you a 'quitter,' a 'camper,' or a 'climber'?" Quitters give up. Campers just sit there and won't try anything new or risky. Then don't take chances. Climbers realize that adversities are a part of life. They don't use excuses. They set goals and move on.

■ Even Gandhi struggled as an adolescent

The compassionate peace-maker Mohandas Gandhi struggled as a young man. According to one encyclopedia, "Gandhi went through a phase of adolescent rebellion, marked by secret atheism, petty thefts, and smoking."

■ Dyslexia didn't stop Charles Schwab

Charles is one of the best known, respected businessmen in the country. He founded one of the biggest discount brokerages in the world. He has dyslexia, a learning disability. Although he struggled with math and reading in school, he worked hard, accepted no excuses, graduated, and started his own successful business.

■ From a sickly child to a "Rough Rider"

As a child, Theodore Roosevelt was very sickly. He had asthma and was very fragile. He loved the outdoors and he credits his "gaining strength" from his many hours outside climbing, hiking, and studying animals and insects. Roosevelt later became president of the United States and was known for his "ruggedness" as an explorer and as the leader of a group of soldiers called the Rough Riders.

Adversity QUIPS

■ Iron Man

Baseball's Cal Ripken, Jr. earned the nickname, "Iron Man" because he went sixteen years without missing a game with the Baltimore Orioles. He played in 2,632 consecutive games! Bumps, bruises, sore muscles, small injuries, and illness didn't stop him from lacing up his shoes and heading out to his position on the field.

■ The world's greatest percussionist

Evelyn Glennie is considered the world's greatest percussionist. She plays piano, clarinet, tam-tams, vibraphone, snare drums, congas, bass drum, temple blocks, cowbells, marimba, cymbals, and several other instruments. Oh, by the way, Evelyn has been profoundly deaf since her early teens!

■ Edgar's rough beginning

Author Edgar Alan Poe had an alcoholic father, his mother died when he was two, and he was abandoned by the rest of his family and relatives.

■ No hand, no-hitter

Jim Abbott was born with no right hand. In 1993, he pitched a no-hitter for the New York Yankees.

■ Mom, I can't walk

Wilma Rudolph was raised in poverty with her 21 brothers and sisters. At the age of four she was struck with pneumonia and scarlet fever, which left her paralyzed in one of her legs. She was unable to walk for a long period of time. Wilma recovered and went on to become the fastest female runner in the world, and in 1960 she won three gold medals in the Olympics.

■ The boxer behind bars

During the 1960's, Rubin 'Hurricane' Carter was one of the top boxers in country. In 1966 he was accused of murder and sent to prison. After twenty years behind bars he was found innocent and released. He overcame the injustices against him and went to help other prisoners who were falsely imprisoned.

Adversity
QUOTES

Adversity
QUOTES

"Adversity has the effect of eliciting talents which in prosperous circumstances would have lain dormant."

-Horace

☞**PRIMING THE PUMP:** Can you think of time you faced an adversity or big challenge and you were surprised at how well you handled it? What happened? Which talents emerged? Explain how overcoming adversities can make one a stronger, more confident individual.

"Strength does not come from winning. Your struggles develop your strengths. When you go through hardships and decide not to surrender, that is strength."

-Arnold Schwarzenegger

☞**PRIMING THE PUMP:** Is one's true strength more likely to appear after winning or losing? Explain your response. Throughout history there have been numerous men and women who faced hardships and failed to surrender. Can you think of one? What hardships did they face and what accomplishments did they eventually achieve?

"Although the world is full of suffering, it is also full of the overcoming it."
-Helen Keller

☞**PRIMING THE PUMP:** Think of a country or group of people in the world today that is suffering, and think of a few things that could be done to ease the suffering. When you watch a news program on television about the millions of children dying of hunger in Africa, and you see the suffering children, how do you react? What are some things you do to help needy people? In the world today there is a lot of suffering: war, AIDS, poverty, hunger, and drug abuse. Will things get better or worse? Are you an optimist or pessimist? Explain you response.

"Worry does not empty tomorrow of its sorrow; it empties today of its strength."
-Corrie Ten Boom

☞**PRIMING THE PUMP:** Explain how worry can empty one's strength. How do you handle your worries? If you worry too much, how can that affect your health? How do you help someone who seems to worry too much? Is a little bit of worrying o.k.? Explain.

"My mother taught me very early to believe I could achieve any accomplishment I wanted to. The first was to walk without braces."
-Wilma Rudolph

☞**PRIMING THE PUMP:** Please read the "QUIP" in this section (Adversity) about Wilma Rudolph. Explain how important her mother's encouragement must have been. What role did 'patience' play in Wilma's recovery? Explain how Wilma's adversity (unable to walk) could have fueled her desire to become a great athlete. Do you believe people like Wilma are more appreciative of their God-given abilities to walk, see, hear, and talk than those who have never lost those abilities?

"I like added pressure. It makes me work harder."
-Mary Lou Retton

☞**PRIMING THE PUMP:** Olympic gymnast, Mary Lou Retton states that pressure makes her work harder. How does pressure affect you as you work on personal goals? What messages does your body give you when you start experiencing too much pressure? What kinds of advice would you give friends who may be putting too much pressure on themselves?

Adversity QUOTES

"Look at me! Look at my arms! I have ploughed and planted. And ain't I a woman? I could work as much and eat as much as a man, when I could get it, and ain't I a woman?"

-Sojourner Truth

☞**PRIMING THE PUMP:** After escaping many years of slavery, Sojourner Truth worked to free more slaves and then she focused on women's suffrage (voting). What adversities did she likely face in her struggle to help women get the right to vote? Can you think of a few possible reasons some women like Sojourner Truth were not "content" with gaining just one right (freedom from slavery), they wanted even more? List several reasons why Sojourner Truth should be admired by people today.

"The good thing about adversity is that it teaches one to learn how to handle more adversity."

-Isabel Martin Williams

☞**PRIMING THE PUMP:** What are some reasons why a second encounter with adversity may be easier to handle than the first one? Can you think of something that might be considered an adversity to one person, but not to another? Is it possible to go through life without ever facing an adversity? Please explain your answer. Some adversities are not our fault, but some might be. What are some things people do that can create personal adversities?

Adversity
QUOTES

"Many of my disappointments have turned out to be blessings in disguise. So whenever anything bad happens to me, I kind of sit back and feel, well, if I give this enough time, it'll turn out this was good, so I don't worry about it too much."
-William Gaines

☞**PRIMING THE PUMP:** Describe a situation in which something bad happened to you, but later on it turned out to be a good thing. Have you ever experienced the opposite? In other words, something good happened to you but later on it turned out to be a bad thing. What happened? How might finishing second in a contest or sporting event be a good thing?

"Even when the horizon seems shrouded in darkness, the hope of a brighter beginning is always in sight."
-Condoleezza Rice

☞**PRIMING THE PUMP:** What are some things you do to lift your spirits when you've had a run of bad luck? Think of a few reasons why it is important to avoiding sulking for a long period of time after a setback? How does one's attitude influence him or her in the search for a brighter beginning?

"We have no right to ask when a sorrow comes, 'Why did this happen to me?' unless we ask the same question for every joy that comes our way."
-Philip E. Bernstein

☞**PRIMING THE PUMP:** What are some possible reasons many people focus on the bad things in life instead of the good? On a piece of paper, make two columns. In column 1, list all the "bad" things that have happened to you in the last month. In column 2, list all the good things that have occurred in your life during the past month. Which list is longer? Share your list with a friend.

Adversity
QUICK STARTERS

- *Three Finger Mordecai*
- *Pastor Umberto*
- *Rama's Trained Mongooses*

THREE FINGER MORDECAI

When Mordecai Brown was a young boy growing up on a small farm in Indiana in the 1880's, he loved to play baseball. He had a dream of playing the major leagues. At the age of five he caught his right hand (his throwing hand) in a piece of farm machinery. In pain, he pulled his hand out, but it was too late; he lost half of his right index finger. A year later he fell while chasing a pig. This time he broke two fingers on his injured right hand. The two fingers never set properly. They were always stiff and crooked. His dream of being a pitcher in the majors went out the window, or did it?

Mordecai tried gripping a baseball. It was a difficult and painful task. He began to squeeze apples, oranges, and other round objects in order to improve his grip. Eventually he was able to start throwing again.

At the age of fifteen he got a job and went to work in coal mines, but he still tried to play baseball. He started playing ball with several local teams at night and on the weekends. He continued to practice pitching, but because of his crooked fingers, he couldn't throw the ball straight; it jumped around. He finally got a chance to pitch a game with his friends. They couldn't hit his pitches because the ball moved around so much, even more than a curve ball.

Thanks to his hand injuries, he developed an almost "un-hittable" pitch and he made it to the majors. He won 272 games and ended up in the Baseball Hall of Fame! At his retirement party he said, "That old paw served me pretty well in its time. It gave me a firmer grip on the ball, so I could spin it over the hump. It gave me a greater dip."

PASTOR UMBERTO

A friend of mine traveled to Costa Rica in 2004 on a mission trip. He came back with many stories, but the one that caught my attention was about an amazing man known as Pastor Umberto. His story is another great example of overcoming adversity. The following comes from a letter my friend sent me while still on the mission trip.

While we worked we got to know some of the villagers a little better. It was fun trying to communicate with one another. Everyone was so appreciative of the fact that we had come so far just to do something that would be a blessing to them. It was very humbling. Most humbling and inspiring, however, was the testimony of Pastor Umberto. Umberto, about eight years ago, had a giant tree fall on him up in the mountains. He was pinned in a sitting position for almost four hours before his friend could return with help and enough strength to remove it. As a result, Umberto lost the use of his lower body and has been paralyzed from the waist down ever since. After going through a brief period of depression God restored his joy and gave him a passion for life that I have never seen in another human being. For years, Umberto used a pulley and a rope (attached to a tree) to hoist himself onto his donkey so he could go and minister to other people. The village is currently raising money to buy him a Suzuki Sidekick that is equipped for someone who is disabled. As I mentioned already, Pastor Umberto is probably the happiest person I ever met. He is always smiling and often shouts out things like, " HALLELUJAH," just out of the blue.

RAMA'S TRAINED MONGOOSES

Rama was a young boy growing up in India in the late 1920's. At that time, all people were part of the caste system. The caste system arranged mankind in a hierarchy of groups of different worth. Caste was hereditary and non-transferable. At the top were the elite Brahmans, and at the bottom were the extremely poor known as the Untouchables.

Rama and his family members were Untouchables. They lived in a small shack just outside the large city of Delhi. His father was a street sweeper, and his mother cleaned toilets at a large hotel. Because his parents worked long hours, he was often left alone, so he would sneak out of town to observe and catch wild animals. He became fascinated with mongooses and he heard numerous stories how they attacked and killed cobras. The mongoose is a furry, weasel-type creature that grows about 18 inches in length. The mongoose hates snakes. When one confronts a snake, it deliberately induces the snake to strike and then pounces on the snake's head from above, cracking the skull with one bite.

During this time in India, the sport of golf was growing in popularity. Golf turned out to be rather dangerous in the Delhi area because many of the courses were located in cobra belts. Several golfers were killed by the dangerous snakes when they went looking for golf balls in the deep grass. Soon the high members of the caste system hired Untouchables to search for lost balls. Two of Rama's uncles were killed when they hunted balls for the rich golfers.

Rama was a very intelligent and creative boy. He soon began to think of ways to earn money to help his poor parents. He believed his avenue to success centered on mongooses. He began to capture them in the wild and kept them in boxes. Then he would sneak onto the golf courses at night and find balls. Next, he started to train his mongooses to travel on a string. Rama would put a mongoose on a string, throw a ball in the deep grass, and then coach the mongoose to enter the grass to check for cobras, before he retrieved the ball.

Soon Rama had several trained mongooses. Many golfers found their way to his shack to purchase them. For the next several years Rama captured and trained hundreds of mongooses. Although his family could not move up in the strict caste system, they did, thanks to Rama, earn enough money to get a better house and avoid the worst levels of poverty.

Anger

QUIPS

Anger
QUIPS

■ Where's that penguin?

Columnist Joe Moore says, "It is impossible to look at a penguin and feel angry."

■ Singing duels diffuse anger

In Greenland, disputes are solved through singing duels. The quibbling parties face off and proceed to sing songs that are filled with insults. While spectators pass the final judgment on the event, the singing generally diffuses the anger, and the dueling parties leave as friends.
–*Mental Floss*, August 2004.

■ Let's shake hands

Indira Gandhi reminds us, "You cannot shake hands with a clinched fist."

■ Fighting fire with fire

"When tempted to 'fight fire with fire,' remember that the fire department usually uses water."
–S.I. Hayakawa

■ Yoga classes required

A Texas judge created a bit of sensation when he sentenced a man who had pushed his wife to take yoga classes as part of his one-year probation. The judge thought the yoga classes would help him control his anger.

■ Winning without fighting

Hundreds of years ago, the Taoist sage Sun-tzu wrote, "For to win 100 victories in 100 battles is not the acme of skill. To subdue the enemy without fighting is the acme of skill."

■ Chew the anger away

One of the best and easiest strategies to help burn off your anger is to chew a piece of sugarless gum. Always keep some handy!

Anger QUIPS

■ Cursed

Of all bad things by which
Mankind are cursed,
Their own bad tempers surely
Are the worst.
      -Richard Cumberland

■ Forgiveness

Much research has been conducted during the past few years that tell us that forgiveness can diminish angry feelings, hostile behaviors, and aggression. Learn to say, "I forgive you."

■ Don't forget compassion

Acclaimed scholar and peace activist Thich Nhat Hanh believes, "Nothing can heal anger except compassion."

■ Skipping wipes out anger

The next time you get angry, start skipping. Skipping, like you did when very young, usually brings a smile to your face.

■ Friend repellent

Question: Do you know one of the best ways to keep friends at a distance?
Answer: Be angry all the time.

■ Don't 'fly off the handle'

To fly off the handle is to lose one's composure and become uncontrollably angry. In her book, *Verbivore's Feast*, Chrysti Smith tells us how the term originated.

> *The 'handle' in this expression belongs to an axe whose head has detached, becoming a dangerous, hurtling missile. Early American axes were often crudely made. Sometimes Eastern manufacturers shipped only the axe heads, and recipients fashioned their own handles. If the homemade handles were not crafted carefully enough to keep the head secure, the chopping blade would sooner or later part company with the handle and fly through the air with a potentially deadly mission—often hitting an innocent person.*

Anger
QUOTES

Anger QUOTES

"He who retains his anger overcomes his greatest enemy."

-Latin proverb

☞**PRIMING THE PUMP:** How can one's anger become his or her enemy? What strategies, inventions, and tricks do you use to help you retain your anger? What are some appropriate ways you vent your anger? Can you think of a time when you did not retain your anger? What negative consequences occurred when you "lost it?"

"Anger gains strength by repetition."

-Swami Sivananda

☞**PRIMING THE PUMP:** How does anger gain strength by repetition? What are some positive activities you can do often (repeat) that can help weaken anger? What serious trouble can someone get in to if his anger has become too strong? How can you tell if your anger is too strong?

"Most anger events (about 70%) are reported to involve people who 'love' or 'like' each other."

-Howard Kassinove

☞**PRIMING THE PUMP:** Do you agree with Kassinove's statistic? Explain your response. What are some possible reasons we often get angry with those we care about? If you are angry, what are the advantages of venting with a loved-one instead of a stranger? How understanding and tolerant are you when a friend or family member directs their anger your way? Are you able to forgive those who vent their anger at you?

Anger
QUOTES

"Relationships that do not end peacefully, do not end at all."
-Merrit Malloy

☞**PRIMING THE PUMP:** How important is it to you to end relationships peacefully? Explain your answer? How do you feel when you end a relationship with an old friend with angry words? Was there ever a time you ended a relationship on "bad terms" that bothered you so much that you had to call the person to seek closure? What happened? When you wish to end a relationship, is it easier for you to write a letter or talk 'face-to-face?' Explain your response.

"Anger cannot be overcome by anger. If a person shows anger to you, and you respond with anger, the result is disastrous. In contrast, if you control anger and show opposite attitudes—compassion, tolerance, and patience—then not only do you yourself remain in peace, but the other's anger will gradually diminish."
-The Dalai Lama

☞**PRIMING THE PUMP:** If you observe two very angry people arguing, how does the event usually end? Is there a 'winner' and 'loser'? When two angry, shouting, threatening individuals are arguing, do you think there is any 'real' listening going on? When confronted by an angry person, how might things 'calm down' if you were to say things like, "I can tell you are angry. I'm sorry you feel that way. Tell me more about it.'? Explain what role facial expressions have in arguments?

"When you make another suffer, he or she will try to find relief by making you suffer."
-Thich Nhat Hanh

☞**PRIMING THE PUMP:** Have you ever been so angry at someone that you wanted to hurt their feelings and make them suffer? If you returned their anger, how did it make you feel? When someone directs their anger at you and then you return the anger, how will that help resolve the conflict? Do you know people who" enjoy" being angry? In what ways do angry people suffer?

Q 36

Anger
QUOTES

"In the midst of great joys do not promise anyone anything. In the midst of great anger do not answer anyone's letter."

-Chinese proverb

☞**PRIMING THE PUMP:** Explain why you might regret writing and sending a letter to someone when you are full of anger? Have you ever emailed or written a letter to someone with whom you were angry, and then later wished you hadn't? What happened? If you receive an angry letter from someone, should you immediately reply or wait for a while to calm down? Explain your answer.

"To carry a grudge is like being stung to death by one bee."

-William H. Walton

☞**PRIMING THE PUMP:** What is a grudge? Explain why holding a grudge can be more harmful to you than the person for whom you are angry? Can you think of a quick, simple thing you could do that would rid you from holding a grudge? Physically, how do you feel when someone is holding a grudge against you?

"Anger is born from ignorance and wrong perceptions. You may be the victim of a wrong perception. You may have misunderstood what you heard and what you saw. You may have a wrong idea of what has been said, what has been done."

-Thich Nhat Hanh

☞**PRIMING THE PUMP:** Before you confront someone whom you are angry with, why do you think it would be a good idea to ask yourself this question, "Am I 100% sure?" Have you ever wrongly accused someone of saying something and then later found out you were wrong? How did you feel and did you apologize? What are the dangers of believing everything other students tell you? Have you ever been wrongly accused of saying something? How did you feel and how did you react?

Q 37

Anger
QUOTES

"I learned that bitterness only consumes the vessel that contains it."

-Rubin "Hurricane" Carter

☞**PRIMING THE PUMP:** Rubin Carter, once a famous boxer, was wrongly accused of murder and spent several years in prison. Do you think he had a valid reason for being angry and bitter? Explain your answer. Explain how being bitter can affect your health and your ability to get along with others. How do you handle others who appear bitter? Think of some reasons why a bitter person needs to forgive and move on.

"I have learned through bitter experience the one supreme lesson to conserve my anger, and as heat conserved is transmitted into energy, even so our anger controlled can be transmitted into a power that can move the world."

-Mahatma Gandhi

☞**PRIMING THE PUMP:** What do you think Gandhi means by 'conserving' anger? What are some ways you could use your anger in a positive way to improve your school or neighborhood? Besides Gandhi, can you think of at least one other 'world changer' that used his or her anger to make a difference in the lives of others? How did they accomplish their goal?

Anger
QUOTES

"When we hate someone and we are angry at her, it is because we do not understand her or the circumstances she comes from. By practicing deep looking we realize that if we grew up like her, in her set of circumstances and in her environment, we would be just like her. That kind of understanding removes your anger and suddenly that person is no longer your enemy."

-Thich Nhat Hanh

☞**PRIMING THE PUMP:** When you are angry at someone, do you ever try to put yourself in their shoes? How does that change your way of dealing with them? Do you believe that there are times others may vent their anger on you, but they really aren't angry with you; they are upset with someone or something else? How do you cope with them? Are you able to let them vent without taking it personally? How can you help these people to better handle their anger?

"In fact, anger makes even a handsome person look ugly. I suggested to a friend, who is remorseful about his flashes of anger, that he keep a large mirror facing his office desk. In case the anger-prone person has a lively sense of humor, this mirror-therapy is likely to work."

-Satguru Bodhinatta Veylanswami

☞**PRIMING THE PUMP:** How do you think people's anger would change if they looked in the mirror when they were angry? What do you think about keeping a mirror close by to look in when you get angry? Would it help you? Do you agree with the part of the quote that notes 'anger makes even a handsome face look ugly'?

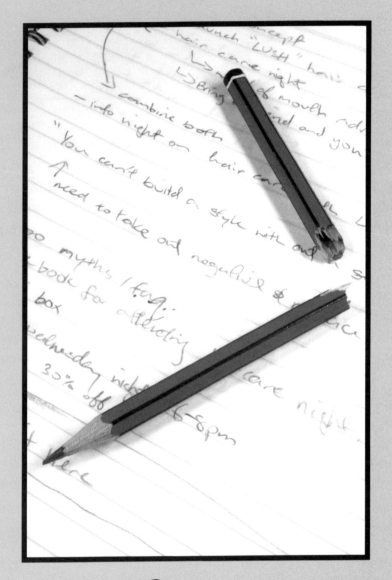

Anger
QUICK STARTERS

- *Good Anger*
- *Running the Anger Away*

QUICK STARTERS

GOOD ANGER

When we hear the word 'anger' we often think of bad things, but anger can also be good. For instance, there are two things that anger me. I am a long distance runner and along the road I see too much litter and too many dogs tethered to trees. I hate litter and I hate to see poor, helpless canines tied up. These two things angered me enough to take action. I have worked with groups and organizations to address these issues. I've written editorials to newspapers and done much to educate students on how they can help. I'm doing my best to utilize my good anger!

Here is another example of good anger. I originally wrote about this lady in my book, *Monday Morning Messages*. Donna Backus is a licensed wildlife rehabilitator who nurses injured animals at her house in Massachusetts. According to a newspaper article I read, she had seen an increase in the number of injured skunks being sent to her home. The reason for this is that skunks love to visit town dumps and landfills, and they were getting their heads caught in discarded Yoplait yogurt cups. The lid on the Yoplait containers had a lip, which acted as a locking devise on the animal's fur. When the skunk backed up, trying to get unstuck, it couldn't get the cup off and they suffocated, got dehydrated, or attacked by other animals. After years of work, phone calls, article-writing, and visits to the Yoplait Company, she was able to convince them to make a larger opening on the cups, thus preventing more skunk deaths.

What are some things happening in society that anger you? What are you going to do about it?

RUNNING THE ANGER AWAY

Andrea always had a problem controlling her anger. In middle school she actually got suspended twice for fighting and she had problems getting along with others. At times she was very defiant toward her parents and teachers. Andrea was referred for counseling. She had numerous counseling sessions with three different counselors, and things didn't improve. One day, when she was very angry, she was sent to the office. The principal was not available so she was sent to see Ms. Harrington, the eighth grade advisor and physical education teacher.

After she finally calmed down, Ms. Harrington told her that she'd noticed how good of a runner she was in physical education class. Ms. Harrington also told her that she could be a very good cross country runner if she put her "gifts and talents" to work. For several days Andrea thought about the encouraging words said by Ms. Harrington. Then one Saturday morning she got up early, had a good breakfast, put on her running shoes, and headed out the door. She made a vow to get up early and run a mile, each day, for ten days. After a week she was "hooked." She loved running. The more she ran, the faster she got. She made the cross country team in ninth grade.

Along the way Andrea noticed that her bouts of anger diminished. Her running gave her self-confidence, helped her burn off anger and frustration, and it gave her time alone to think. Andrea went on to college and finally had a grasp on anger. Hours of counseling didn't help her as much as the hundreds of miles running! Running can run away anger.

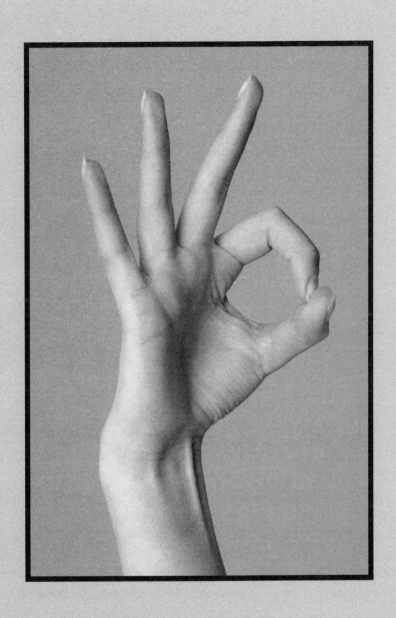

Attitude
QUIPS

Q

Attitude
QUIPS

■ A positive outlook

"Wait 'till next year!" It's the favorite cry of baseball fans, football fans, hockey fans, and gardeners."
–Robert Orben

■ Don't run from problems

Henry David Thoreau encouraged people to go on the offense when he said, "When a dog runs at you, whistle for him."

■ Good advice

Fear less, hope more, whine less,
breathe more; talk less, say more,
hate less, love more,
and all good things are yours.

-Swedish proverb

■ Where's your key?

The Hindu sage, Swami Chinmayananda reminds us, "Don't put the key to happiness in someone else's pocket."

■ Good days

Every day you need to tell yourself, "All days are good, but some are better than others."

■ Donuts and the optimist

Twixt the optimist and pessimist
the difference is droll.
The optimist sees the donut
but the pessimist sees the hole.

-McLandburgh Wilson

■ Two prisoners

Two prisoners looked through steel bars. One saw mud, the other saw stars.

Attitude
QUIPS

■ Stop complaining

Writer, Thomas Fuller notes, "Every horse thinks his own pack heaviest."

■ A Christmas kind of guy

When sports reporter, Joe Garagiola was asked to describe baseball great, Yogi Berra he replied, "He's one of those Christmas Eve guys. There are people like that—every day in their lives is like Christmas Eve."

■ What's your blood type?

Philosopher, Gurudeva describes one of his friends. "I've known a man for many years who is always cheerful, generous, and optimistic. I asked him one day how he maintains such a wonderful outlook on life, he replied, 'It must be my blood; it's B positive.'"

■ Give thanks

When you arise in the morning, give thanks for
the morning light. Give thanks for your life
and strength. Give thanks for your food and
give thanks for the joy of living.
And if perchance you see no reason for giving thanks,
rest assured the fault is in yourself.

-The Gospel of the Redman

■ Corn flakes, juice and affirmations

Every morning at breakfast, repeat at least one affirmation three times to yourself. Affirmations are self-statements that affirm your right as an individual to embrace and achieve the kinds of changes in yourself that you choose to make. Sample affirmations could be, *I know I'll do well on the test. I will refrain from spreading gossip. I will be respectful to my teachers. I will avoid being jealous. I will eat a nutritious meal for lunch.*

Q
45

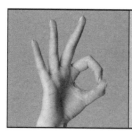

Attitude
QUOTES

"I am an optimist. It does not seem too much use being anything else."
-Winston Churchill

☞**PRIMING THE PUMP:** What is an optimist? What is a pessimist? What makes some people optimistic while others become pessimistic? Do you prefer to be around pessimists or optimists? Explain your response. How do you think being a pessimist can affect one's health? Which one of these two personality types is more likely to achieve personal goals and explain why?

"A lot of people are waiting for Martin Luther King or Mahatma Gandhi to come back, but they are gone. We are it. It is up to us. It is up to you."
-Marian Wright Edelman

☞**PRIMING THE PUMP:** Many people are complainers while others are world-changers. Which one are you? What are some things who've done recently to help your school, neighborhood, or community? What were some things Martin Luther King, Jr. tried to change in the world? What did Gandhi accomplish in his lifetime? Be a dreamer; what are some positive changes you would like to see in the world?

"What is the difference between an obstacle and an opportunity?....Our attitude toward it. Every opportunity has difficulty and every difficulty has an opportunity."
-J. Sidlow Baxter

☞**PRIMING THE PUMP:** Explain how a difficulty or a challenge can turn in to a great opportunity? Think of a famous inventor, activist, political leader, or artist who had to overcome numerous obstacles on their way to success. Who did you think of, and what were some of the obstacles he or she encountered? What has been one of the biggest obstacles you had to face and how did you handle it? Did it make you a stronger person? Are you more resilient now because of it?

Attitude
QUOTES

"I can accept failure, but I cannot accept not trying."
-Michael Jordan

☞**PRIMING THE PUMP:** Are you a risk-taker, willing to try new things? What is one activity you tried and failed at several times before succeeding? What personal traits, skills helped you succeed? How do you handle failures and setbacks?

"Everything may be taken from us except the last of the human freedoms—our ability to choose our own attitude in any situation."
-Victor Frankl

☞**PRIMING THE PUMP:** Frankl believes that no matter the situation, good or bad, we can choose our attitude. Do you agree or disagree, and explain your answer? Think of someone you know personally who has had a tough life but keeps a positive attitude. How does his or her positive attitude and temperament 'rub off' on you? How do you react when you hear an extremely wealthy person complain about little things? How do you react when you see starving children in another country smile and express their appreciation for a small plate of rice?

"When you are obsessed with how people have done you wrong, you have little ambition to change the behavior that got you into the mess"
-Bob Brezny

☞**PRIMING THE PUMP:** When someone has 'done you wrong,' are you able to forgive and move on or do you sulk and complain for a long period of time? What are the disadvantages of spending so much of your time and energy on those who did you wrong? What are some strategies, interventions you have used to help stop obsessing?

Attitude QUOTES

"The guys who don't complain are the toughest. The guys who gripe are always a problem and I've got no time for them."

-Lance Armstrong

☞**PRIMING THE PUMP:** How do you feel being around people who are always complaining? Have you ever been at a party with someone who constantly whined, or complained? How did you cope? How can one player, with a negative attitude, affect the team? If you were a coach, selecting players for your team, what attribute would you most likely consider first, attitude or athletic ability? Explain your answer.

"Everybody thinks of changing humanity and nobody thinks of changing himself."

-Leo Tolstoy

☞**PRIMING THE PUMP:** Before we complain about someone else's attitude, do you think it is important to check ours first? Explain your answer? How do you react when someone accuses you of having a bad attitude? When you encounter a negative person, what are some things you might say or do to help them feel better? When you sense a bad attitude coming on, what do you do to try to stop it?

"No pessimist ever discovered the secrets of the stars, or sailed to an uncharted land, or opened a new heaven to the human spirit."

-Helen Keller

☞**PRIMING THE PUMP:** What are some possible reasons why pessimists seldom accomplish great things? Do you believe pessimists are risk-takers? Explain your response. Think of some reasons why inventors, political leaders, doctors, and scientists need to be optimists?

Attitude
QUOTES

"Each of us makes his own weather, determines the color of the skies in the emotional universe which he inhabits."

-Fulton J. Sheen

☞**PRIMING THE PUMP:** Who do you think is responsible for your emotions, and why? What are your thoughts about this rather popular saying, "If you want to have a good day or bad day, it's your choice?" How do you think the real weather (clouds, sun, rain, snow, heat, cold, etc) affects one's attitude?

"The world is a great mirror. It reflects back to you what you are. If you are loving, if you are friendly, if you are helpful, the world will prove loving and friendly and helpful. The world is what you are."

-Thomas Dreier

☞**PRIMING THE PUMP:** Do you agree or disagree with Dreier's 'mirror' theory? If you encounter a rude waitress, and you return her rudeness, is she likely to change? Explain your response. Have you ever 'really' tried to be kind to a rude person and it didn't help? What happened? If someone refuses to help you, but later on she asks you for help, what will you do?

"When I am flexible and forgiving, I am happy. When I am rigid and righteous, I am unhappy. It's that simple!"

-Hugh Prather

☞**PRIMING THE PUMP:** What does it mean to be flexible when dealing with people who have challenging behaviors and personalities? Have you ever had to adjust your temperament in order to get along with someone? What adjustments did you have to make? What are some possible reasons a person becomes unhappy when he or she remains rigid, unwilling to be flexible?

49

Attitude
QUOTES

"You can vitally influence your life from within by auto-suggestion. The first thing each morning, and the last thing each night, suggest to yourself specific ideas that you wish to embody in your character and personality. Address such suggestions to yourself, silently or aloud, until they are deeply impressed upon your mind."

-Greenville Kleiser

☞**PRIMING THE PUMP:** What is one aspect of your personality or character that you need to improve? What are you presently doing to address your concern? If you do what Greenville Kleiser suggests, state some positive suggestions to yourself each morning and evening, how do you think it will help you improve that one aspect of your personality or character? Have you ever used 'self-talk" before? What was the situation and how did it help?

"The amount of satisfaction you get from life depends largely on your ingenuity, self-sufficiency, and resourcefulness. People who wait around for life to supply their satisfaction usually find boredom instead."

-William Menninger

☞**PRIMING THE PUMP:** Who do you think is mostly responsible for the satisfaction you get from life? What are some advantages of seeking your own satisfaction instead of sitting around and waiting for others to provide excitement and entertainment? When you say, "I'm bored," what do your parents or teachers usually say? If Joey says," I'm bored," whose fault is it? Explain your answer.

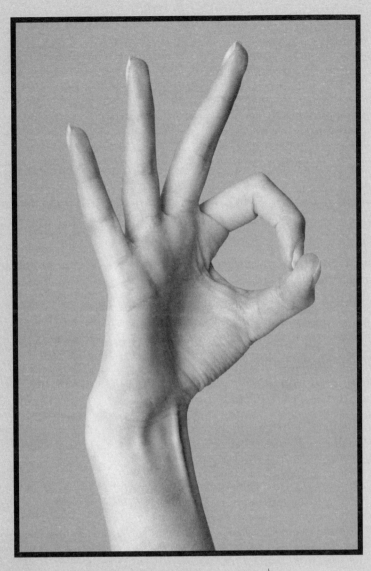

Attitude
QUICK STARTERS

- *The Most Cheerful Member*
- *The Positive Attitude Blueprint*

Q 51

Attitude
QUICK STARTERS

THE MOST CHEERFUL MEMBER

*from the diary of Catherine Haun in 1849 during the great migration west...

To add to the horrors of the surroundings, one man was bitten on the ankle by a rattlesnake. Although every available remedy was tried upon the wound, his limb had to be amputated with the aid of a common handsaw. Fortunately, for him, he had a good, brave wife along who helped and cheered him into health and usefulness; for it was not long before he found much he could do and was not considered a burden, although the woman had to do a man's work as they were alone. He was of a mechanical turn and later on helped mend wagons, yokes, and harnesses. And when the train was on the move he sat in the wagon, gun by his side, and repaired boots and shoes. He was one of the most cheery members of the company and told good stories and sang at the camp fire, putting shame to some of the able bodied who were given to complaining and selfishness.

Attitude
QUICK STARTERS

THE POSITIVE ATTITUDE BLUEPRINT

Following is a blueprint for developing a positive attitude. Look it over and ask yourself, "How am I doing?"

Gratitude: A positive attitude begins with a daily dose of gratitude. Before getting out of bed each morning take time to count your blessings. Be thankful to your country, parents, and teachers for providing love, food, shelter, and freedom. Consider keeping a Gratitude Journal.

Self-talk: Probably the most important conversation you have each day is with yourself. Use positive self-talk. Tell yourself: I'm going to have a good day. My attitude is my choice. I'll study hard. I'll not let rude people mess up my day. I am smart.

Choosing your friends: Remember the old saying, "The friends you keep determine the troubles you'll meet." Who are you hanging with? Can your friend's positive, or negative, attitudes rub off on you?

Kindness: Be kind to others, even if they are unkind to you. If someone is rude to you and you return the rudeness, does that end the problem? The more unkind you are to others, the worse your attitude gets!

Forgiveness: Learn to forgive. Holding grudges, and/or seeking revenge only make you more miserable.

Sleep: You need at least eight hours of sleep every night. A lack of sleep makes you moody, irritable, hard to get along with, and it hurts your academic and athletic performances.

Nutrition: The more healthy your diet, the better you look and feel.

Exercise: Turn off the television, put down that video game, get off the phone, and push yourself away from the computer. Get outdoors. Walk, run, hike, or ride a bike. The more you exercise, the more energy you'll have.

Extra-curricular activities: Busy kids tend to stay out of trouble. Play a sport, learn how to play a musical instrument, join a club, go to church, learn martial arts, and find interesting hobbies.

Service: The best thing to do when you are feeling down is to help others. Help your mother clean the house, stock shelves at the food bank, mow your neighbor's yard, pick up litter, or help the homeless.

Solitude: Find at least an hour a day to be alone in order to recharge your batteries.

Bullying, Teasing, & Gossiping QUIPS

■ Mom. I don't want to go to school today.

Between 150,000 and 200,000 students stay home from school every day to avoid being teased, bullied, or threatened.

■ Aaron's "bully strategy"

The famous television producer, Aaron Spelling had a clever way of handling bullies when he was a kid. Whenever bullies would try to pick a fight, Aaron would just tell them a story and not finish it. He told them he would finish the story the next day and they would let him go home. He would run as fast as he could before they changed their minds.

■ The Wandering Tattler

Did you know there was a bird called the Wandering Tattler? While I describe the bird to you, see if you can notice a resemblance between the bird and those students at school who like to tattle. The Wandering Tattler is a shorebird that summers in Alaska and northwest Canada and winters on the coasts from California to Australia. It is a solitary bird that is seldom seen in groups. It got its name from its annoying, shrieking sounds. The hunters don't like the bird because its call scares away all the other birds. It seems as though this bird is tattling on the hunters. The bird wanders endlessly, and when frightened, will crouch and hide.

■ If only he knew

There was a boy named Timothy Silly. Because of his last named he got teased a lot. His father, who suffered from a mental illness, killed Timothy and then shot himself. Later, friends of Timothy's discovered that the word silly comes from the Latin word selig which means "blessed" or "holy."

■ Beware of the upside down flower

There is a term known as the 'language of flowers,' which gives a meaning to each flower. For instance, a rose means 'love' and hyacinth means 'sorrow.' But, in the old days, if you received a flower upside down, the opposite meaning was intended. Thus if you received tulips with their stems up, it would mean "I don't love you anymore," instead of ones "declaration of love." Years ago young boys and girls would tease each other by sending "upside down" flowers!

Bullying, Teasing, & Gossiping QUIPS

■ Oh, so true!

Do you agree with cowboy philosopher, Will Rogers' well-known quote? He said, "The only time people dislike gossip is when you gossip about them"

■ Does your name determine your fate?

Students often tease peers because of their names. But does having an unusual name mean one will be unsuccessful in life compared to others who have more common names? Check this out! Many years ago a man in New York City had two sons. He named one, Winner and the other, Loser. How do you think they fared in life? Winner was never able to keep a job and had a lengthy criminal record: nearly three dozen arrests for burglary, domestic violence, trespassing, resisting arrest, and more. Loser was an honor student in high school, graduated from college, joined the New York City Police Department and ended up as a sergeant.

■ Tough girls

Former British television personality, Paula Yates had four daughters named, Heavenly Hiraani Tiger Lily, Fifi Trixibelle, Peaches Honeyblossom, and Pixie. Do you think they needed tough skin?

■ The Dirty Thirty

Hal Urban was a high school teacher for many years before becoming an author. In his book, *Positive Words, Powerful Results*, he listed the results of a survey given to many of his students. He asked them to list things that people say that they don't like to hear. He called his list, "The Dirty Thirty." Here are their top ten "dislikes;" Bragging, swearing/gross-out language, gossip, angry words, lies, mean-spirited & hurtful words, judging others, playing 'poor me'—the self-pity game, making discouraging remarks, and embarrassing & humiliating others.

■ Wisdom

"A kind mouth multiplies friends and appeases enemies, and gracious lips prompt friendly greetings."
-Wisdom of Sirach

■ Goody Two Shoes

Elementary students who behave well are usually very popular; they have many friends. By middle school many of these same students get teased for being "too" good. They are often labeled, goody two shoes. Goody Two Shoes was the name of a character from an old nursery rhyme written by Oliver Goldsmith. The heroine was a poor, kind child who had only one shoe. When she eventually got a matching pair, she jumped for joy and whenever she met someone she would point to her little feet and shout, "Two shoes!"

■ Good gossip

Years ago, gossip was considered good. The word 'gossip' originally implied a spiritual relationship. A gossip was a sponsor at a baptism, one who spoke on behalf of the child and who provided spiritual guidance to the child as it grew. A gossip could be a godmother or godfather. Gossiping was speech within the community that was positive in nature. So, in the old days, gossips spread good news. Today's gossips usually spread bad news.

■ Chickens & Children

Philosopher Thomas Fuller noted, "Children and chickens must be always pickin'"

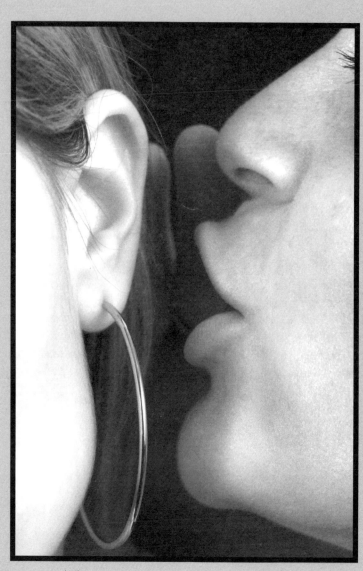

Bullying, Teasing, & Gossiping
QUOTES

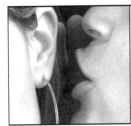

Bullying, Teasing, & Gossiping
QUOTES

"Whoever gossips to you will gossip of you."

-Spanish proverb

☞**PRIMING THE PUMP:** Tell why you agree or disagree with this proverb. Can you think of a time someone, who you thought was a good friend, spread gossip about you? How did you handle it? Have you ever been guilty of spreading gossip? How did that make you feel?

"Let us keep our mouths shut and our pens dry until we know the facts."

-A. J. Carlson

☞**PRIMING THE PUMP:** Have you ever heard some gossip that was so "hot" you couldn't wait to tell others? Did you get burned? In other words, did you find out later that the gossip was not true? How did you feel? Have you ever been a victim of untrue gossip? How did you feel and how did you handle it?

"What you don't see with your eyes, don't invent with your tongue."

-Jewish proverb

☞**PRIMING THE PUMP:** Do you believe everything you hear from your peers? Why not? Do you believe that some students "make-up" lies to hurt others? Think of some reasons why students do that.

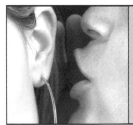
"Part of the happiness of life consists not in fighting battles, but in avoiding them. A masterly retreat is in itself a victory."

-Norman Vincent Peale

☞**PRIMING THE PUMP:** Are you learning to avoid negative people? How do you do it? What are some strategies you use when you encounter someone who teases or bullies you? Do you consider it a sign of strength or weakness when you go out of your way to avoid rude people? Explain your response.

"What Peter tells me about Paul tells me more about Peter than it does about Paul."

-Ruth Anne Crouse

☞**PRIMING THE PUMP:** What can you learn about one's character by how they talk about others? If you hear a classmate saying something rude or untrue about your best friend, what do you do? When you hear someone saying unkind things about another person, do you stay and listen or walk away? Think of a reason or two why it might be best to walk away. Do rude people enjoy having an audience around them while they gossip? What "message" are you giving rude people by hanging around and listening to them?

"Developing mind-mouth harmony is the greatest skill in the world, because if you make a mistake with either, you can find yourself in serious personal danger."

-George Thompson

☞**PRIMING THE PUMP:** Can you think of a time you said something you wished later on that you hadn't? What happened? Can you think of a situation where, even though someone is being rude to you, you might be better off keeping your mouth closed? Have you ever witnessed a situation where someone got hurt, or got into serious trouble because he or she "didn't" keep his/her mouth closed?

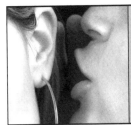

Bullying, Teasing, & Gossiping
QUOTES

"As you would not bark back at a dog, do not waste your time arguing with foolish people."

-Sage Yogaswami

☞**PRIMING THE PUMP:** Have you ever entered into a discussion with someone who was being so unreasonable that it seemed like you were wasting your time talking to them? What did you do? When people argue, do you really think they listen to each other? What are some strategies you use when exiting a conversation with an extremely unreasonable person?

"Ducks quack and humans gossip. If you don't quack, the other ducks will run off. If you don't gossip, you're going to have very short conversations."

-Hugh Prather

☞**PRIMING THE PUMP:** Do gossiping people draw a crowd? Think of a few reasons why that happens? If students never gossiped, would conversations be shorter? How do you think some of your peers feel about you if you don't engage in gossip? Will you gain more trust and respect from your friends if you don't engage in gossip? Explain.

"If I really liked myself, I wouldn't do anything to hurt myself or do anything to hurt others."

-Sid Simon

☞**PRIMING THE PUMP:** Is it possible that when someone is feeling down, he may tease others to make himself feel better? Explain. Are happy, successful people less apt to tease, bully, or gossip? In the past it was believed that bullies had low self-esteem, now recent research finds that many bullies have high self-esteem. What are your thoughts about that?

Q 61

Bullying, Teasing, & Gossiping

QUICK STARTERS

- The Barber Saint
- Nickels & Dimes
- Lessons Learned from a 'Pea-brain'
- Tommy's Got a Bald Momma!

THE BARBER SAINT

If you visit small town barber shops and hair salons these days you'll be sure to hear a great deal of gossip. Many "receivers" of gossip like pass it on, but there was one barber who refused to pass along unkind words. Let me tell you about the Barber Saint.

Pierre Toussaint was born a black, humble slave in Haiti in 1776 and eventually elevated to the status of "Venerable" by the Pope in 1996. Pierre's kind master, Jean Berard, taught him how to read and write. Pierre moved with Berard to New York in 1787 where he learned the trade of barbering. Pierre opened his own barber shop where he gained a reputation for being honest and trustworthy. Unlike many of his fellow barbers, he refused to spread gossip, even though many of his customers shared interesting, and sometimes 'alarming' bits of information. Pierre had an unusual approach for dealing with gossip. Instead of passing on the negative talk, he would add their concerns to his growing prayer list. Yes, he prayed for the gossipers and for the victims of their hurtful words!

Later in life he opened a home for orphans and the poor. He worked hard to free other slaves, opened a school for black children, and set up a religious order for black women. According to author, Parminder Summon in his book, *Saints & Sinners*, "Toussaint never allowed his poverty to rob him of his dignity. He rose above racist slurs and ignorant attitudes….he didn't perform miracles, write great books….he didn't know the benefits of privileged birth, but experienced the depths of a generous heart."

Pierre Toussaint refused to pass on the gossip he heard. How about you? Can you do anything to stop the gossip train?

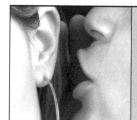

Bullying, Teasing, & Gossiping
QUICK STARTERS

NICKLES & DIMES

Larry was the new kid in class. He was a very quiet, shy boy. Almost immediately, Hollis, the first grade bully, targeted him. Whenever the teacher wasn't around, Hollis was extremely mean to Larry and he liked to embarrass him in front of others. One of his favorite tricks to play on Larry had to deal with nickels and dimes.

On the playground he would gather his buddies and say, "Watch this." Hollis would call to Larry, "Hey come here!" Hollis would take out a nickel and dime and say, "Larry, which coin do you want?" Larry always took the nickel. As he walked away, Hollis and the other kids laughed because he always took the larger- sized coin! As Hollis laughed he would say, "What a dummy. Larry takes the nickel because it's bigger so he thinks must be worth more." Hollis played this trick numerous times and Larry always took the nickel.

During the last month of school the teacher finally witnessed one of Hollis' bully sessions with Larry. She was surprised that Larry, once again, took the nickel. Later she talked with him and asked, "How long has Hollis been bullying you and why do you always take the nickel? You know a dime is worth more." Larry replied, "Yes, I know a dime is worth more, but if I took the dime, Hollis wouldn't play the trick on me anymore. I now have a jar full of nickels and I've got enough to buy that model airplane I've been wanting."

Larry out-smarted the bully! Sometimes you've got to get creative when dealing with bullies.

LESSONS LEARNED FROM A 'PEA-BRAIN'

When I was in second grade there was a boy named Timothy who loved to tease me. It all started one day when I gave a silly answer to a teacher's question and he called me a, "Pea-brain." That became my nickname. Every morning he would greet me with, "Hey, Pea-brain!" After calling me the name for a few weeks, he advanced to his next level of teasing. Whenever we had peas for lunch, he would bring a few back to class. He threw the peas at me, put them on my seat, and once he stuck one in my ear. Timothy was sneaky; he never got caught. No matter how many times I told on him, he denied doing it. Things got so upsetting to me that as soon as the teacher passed out the monthly lunchroom menu, I would look to see which days peas were to be served. On those days I used to pretend that I was sick so I could stay home and avoid Timothy's pea tricks.

By the middle of the school year things got worse. Nobody helped me. Then one day a thought came to me. I realized that I couldn't change Timothy, I could only change myself. Maybe if I changed, then he might change. So, I came up with the following five- step plan.

- I would stop tattling on him.

- I would become invitational. I invited him to sit with me at lunch, be on my kickball team, and to work at my table in class.

- I would stick-up for him if anyone accused him of something or if anyone teased him.

- I would say at least three nice things to him every day.

- I would find what interests/hobbies we had in common. I discovered that he and I both collected baseball cards and soon we spent much time together talking about cards and trading them.

By the end of the school year we were best of friends. I learned a valuable lesson; you can't change others, you can only change yourself, but when you change, they change!

TOMMY'S GOT A BALD MOMMA!

There was a ten-year-old boy named Tommy Hansen that lived in an old, small house in the country. He kept to him self and didn't seem to have any close friends. Every day he appeared to be in a hurry to get home and see his mother. Seldom was he seen outdoors playing. None of the kids in his class or on his bus ever saw his mother. He ignored questions about his mother.

One day a boy in his class named Joe saw Tommy and his mother on their front porch. Joe couldn't believe what he saw; Tommy's mother was bald! He couldn't wait to tell everyone. The next morning on the bus Joe started teasing Tommy. Joe and his friends starting shouting, "Tommy's got a bald momma!" The chant went on for several minutes until Tommy couldn't take it anymore. He got up, walked to the back of the bus and punched Joe. The two boys fought for several minutes before the driver broke it up. The boys ended up in the principal's office.

The principal called both parents to school. As Joe waited in the office, he saw Tommy's mother walk very slowly into the office. She appeared weak and slightly bent over. Then he saw her bald head, and started to giggle. Then the principal came out to greet her. She and the principal went into his office and closed the door. Joe leaned up against the door trying to hear what they were saying. Then he heard something that made him sick to his stomach. The principal said, "I'm sorry I had to call you in Mrs. Hansen. I know you've been ill with all the chemotherapy lately." Joe now realized why she was bald and why Tommy got so upset; she had cancer.

Joe returned to his seat next to Tommy. He held out his hand and said, "I'm sorry. Please forgive me, I didn't know."

Career

QUIPS

Career QUIPS

■ Scratch it

Poet and author, Laurie Beth Jones, encourages us to, "Find a niche and scratch it."

■ Pace yourself

Whatever career you choose, pace yourself; mix work with some relaxation. When author Jack London visited Hawaii to write he promised himself to write only a thousand words a day. When he reached that limit he would throw down his pencil and say, "We'll, my job's done for today!"

■ Fast runners

When the well-known long distance runner Kip Lagat, from Kenya, was asked why his country produces so many fast runners, he stated, "It's the road signs that read, BEWARE OF LIONS!"

■ MJ missed more than he made

Michael Jordan is considered by many to be the greatest basketball player of all time. But did you know that during his successful career he missed more shots than he made? He attempted 24,537 shots and made 12,192 baskets. That gave him a career shooting percentage of 49.7%. He was a great free throw shooter though, making about 85% of his free throws.

■ A second opinion

Speaking of Michael Jordan; during his stretch of winning six NBA championships, his coach was Phil Jackson. Jackson is one of the all time greatest coaches. After his years as an NBA player he wanted to be a coach but couldn't get a job. Eventually he went for career counseling and took a test that looked at his skills, desires, and talents. Check this out! When the results came back, the top two vocations suggested by his personality profile were: housekeeper and trail guide!

■ Would you apply for this job?

WANTED: Young, skinny, wiry fellows, not over 18.
Must be expert riders, willing to risk death daily.
Orphans preferred. Wages: $25 a week.
-Pony Express
Nebraska, 1860

Career
QUIPS

■ From unemployed to a millionaire

In 1949, Jack Wrum, who was jobless at the time, picked up a bottle on a beach near San Francisco. Inside was the following message that had been placed in the bottle twelve years earlier by the eccentric sewing machine heiress, Daisy Singer Alexander.

> *To avoid any confusion, I leave my entire estate to the lucky person who finds this bottle, and to my attorney, Barry Cohen, share and share alike.*
>
> -Daisy Singer Alexander, June 20, 1937

■ Finally, "Lady Principal"

In the 1890's, Sue May Kirkland was a school teacher who eventually became a principal in North Carolina. Although she was a principal, her exact job titles changed frequently. Here were some of her titles: Custodian of Manners and Morals, Supervisor of Habits and Manners, Referee in Matters Social and Domestic, and finally, Lady Principal.

■ Practicing to be a barber

John Tayman's book, *The Colony*, told the plight of people with leprosy who were exiled to a remote Hawaiian island. Many lepers went blind, but they were still determined to be productive residents. Many of them volunteered to let a practicing barber cut their hair. The barber-in-training, Kenso Seki noted, "So if I make a mistake cutting, they don't worry."

Career
QUIPS

■ Being early leads to a career

Ibrahim Hussein, from Kenya, won the New York City Marathon once and the Boston Marathon three times. When asked how he got to be such a great runner he said, "At my school my teacher asked me to be the timekeeper. It was my responsibility to make sure the other students were on time. So it was important that I arrived first."

■ Ten hardest things to do in sports

Are you thinking of a career in sports? The USA TODAY sports staff determined these are the ten hardest things to do in sports:

#1: Hitting a baseball

#2: Driving a race car at great speeds around a track

#3: Pole vaulting at heights over 15 feet

#4: Hitting a golf ball long and straight

#5: Returning a 130-mile per hour serve in tennis

#6: Landing a quad in figure skating

#7: Running a marathon

#8: Riding in the Tour de France

#9: Stopping a soccer penalty kick

#10: Skiing downhill at 80-90 miles per hour

Career

QUOTES

Career
QUOTES

"We should all do what, in the long run, gives us joy, even if it is only picking grapes or sorting the laundry."

-E. B. White

☞**PRIMING THE PUMP:** List a few reasons why it is important to have a job you enjoy. What are a few careers that you believe you would enjoy? Think of the last time you witnessed someone doing a job that they obviously did not enjoy. How could you tell they were unhappy? How can one's job affect one's personal health? If find yourself in a job you no longer enjoy, what would you do?

"If you have to support yourself, you had better well find something that is going to be interesting."

-Katherine Hepburn

☞**PRIMING THE PUMP:** Think of two or three jobs that you would find to be very boring. What are a few jobs that you would find to be very interesting? Is it possible for two people to have the same job, and one finds it boring while the other person finds it very interesting? How can that be? Can you think of a time in your life when you may have to temporarily take a somewhat boring, routine job?

"If a man is called to be a street sweeper, he should sweep streets even as Michelangelo painted, or Beethoven composed music, or Shakespeare wrote poetry. He should sweep streets so well that all the hosts of heaven and earth will pause to say, here lived a great street sweeper who did his job well."

-Martin Luther King, Jr.

☞**PRIMING THE PUMP:** Think of a few reasons why it is important to do every job in such a way that you can feel proud of your effort. When you apply for a job, do you think the employer will seek references from your earlier jobs? If so, what kinds of positive things would you want your past employers to say about you? When you visit a restaurant, which kind of waitress would you prefer wait on you, the one who is slow, careless and rude, or the waitress that is swift, friendly, and seems to like her job? Explain you reasons.

Q 72

Career
QUOTES

"Starting out to make money is the greatest mistake if life. Do what you feel you have a flair for doing, and if you are good enough at it, the money will come."

-Greer Garson

☞**PRIMING THE PUMP:** What are some negative consequences of selecting a job solely based on a high salary? Can you think of a couple professions that start out with a low salary but have great earnings potential? What is a career that you would consider, even though it may never be high paying? For what reasons would you select that career? Can you think of an adult or two who have high paying jobs but aren't happy? What careers did they choose?

"Give me a man who sings at work."

-Thomas Carlyle

☞**PRIMING THE PUMP:** If you were an employer, for what reasons would you want employees that sing at work? Do you think employees who whistle and sing on the job could me more productive than those who don't? Explain your response. What are a few chores, jobs, or tasks that you do in which you might whistle or sing while doing them? What are a few chores, jobs, or tasks you do in which you may never whistle or sing while doing them?

"The power I exert on the court depends on the power of my arguments, not my gender."

-Sandra Day O'Connor

☞**PRIMING THE PUMP:** As long as the person is effective, should gender make a difference? Explain your response. What are your thoughts on choosing a career that is overly-represented by the opposite gender? For instance, if you are a male, would you consider nursing, or, if you are a female, would you consider being a police officer? What are some pros and cons of choosing such careers?

Career QUOTES

"If the career you have chosen has some unexpected inconvenience, console yourself by reflecting that no career is without them."

-Jane Fonda

☞**PRIMING THE PUMP:** Can you think of any profession that is without an occasional hassle? How can inconveniences in your job help you to grow as a person? How can inconveniences enhance you creativity? Interview a few adults and have them share a few hassles that come with their jobs and ask them how they deal with them.

"If I wanted to be a tramp, I would seek information and advice from the most successful tramp I could find. If I wanted to become a failure, I would seek advice from men who have never succeeded. If I wanted to succeed in all things I would look around a lot for those who are succeeding, and do as they have done."

-Joseph Marshall Wade

☞**PRIMING THE PUMP:** If you decided to become a teacher, who would you seek out for advice and why? If you associate with positive, successful individuals, how can that help lead you to success? Can associating with negative, unsuccessful individuals bring you down? How?

"I studied the lives of great men and famous women, and I found that the men and women who got to the top were those who did their jobs they had in hand with everything they had with energy and enthusiasm and hard work."

-Harry S. Truman

☞**PRIMING THE PUMP:** For what reasons do you think energy and enthusiasm are important ingredients for success? How was energy and enthusiasm critical for the success of great athletes like Lance Armstrong and Venus and Serena Williams? What activities do you engage in that help recharge your batteries so you have the energy needed to be successful in school and life?

Career
QUOTES

"Careers, like rockets, don't always take off on schedule. The key is to keep working on the engine."

-Gary Sinise

☞**PRIMING THE PUMP:** On the pathway to your selected career, what types of setbacks might you encounter? Explain how it is possible for some people to have several careers in a lifetime? Is it possible to have several different jobs in a lifetime but, still have the same career? Explain your response. What are some possible disadvantages of climbing the career ladder too quickly? Can you explain the difference between a job and a career?

"I have always been driven to buck the system, to innovate, to take things beyond where they've been."

-Sam Walton

☞**PRIMING THE PUMP:** Sam Walton was the founder of Walmart and was known for being innovative and for being a risk-taker. Can you think of any other famous people who took risks on their way to success? What did they do? Do you consider yourself a risk-taker? Explain your response. What are some activities in which you engage that enhance your creativity and ability to be innovative?

"When I was young, I said to God, 'God, tell me the mystery of the universe.' But God answered, 'That knowledge is reserved for me alone.' So I said, 'God, tell me the mystery of the peanut.' Then God said, 'Well, George, that's more nearly your size.' And he told me."

-George Washington Carver

☞**PRIMING THE PUMP:** George Washington Carver became an expert on the peanut. Thanks to him, how many uses do you know for the peanut? Do you believe that everyone is born with special gifts and talents that can lead to their career? What gifts or talents do you have that may help you in your career choice? What are you presently doing to enhance your special gifts?

75

Career
QUOTES

"I hope whatever you choose to do; you will love what you're doing. Because, if you are passionate about what you do, there will be no limit to what you can achieve and no limit to the difference you can make."

-Elaine Chao

☞**PRIMING THE PUMP:** What does the word 'passionate' mean to you? How can you tell when someone is passionate about something? What is at least one thing for which you are passionate? Can people truly be happy and successful in life without passion? Explain. If you were an employer, list two or three reasons why you would like for your employees to be passionate about their jobs.

Career
QUICK STARTERS

- *The Shy Mathematician*
- *Four Authors' Success Stories*
- *Louisa May Alcott's Advice to Promising Young Authors*

THE SHY MATHEMATICIAN

In the November, 2005 issue of *Psychology Today*, Peter Doskoch and Carlin Flora tell of an amazing, somewhat shy mathematician named Andrew Wiles. When Andrew was a young boy he became very interested in math; he especially liked solving tough problems. When he was ten years old he first heard of Fermat's Last Theorem, a seemingly simple problem that had stumped mathematicians for 350 years! The problem was devised by a French mathematician named Pierre de Fermat. Andrew remembers what he thought when he first saw the problem. He said, "It looked so simple, and yet all the great mathematicians in history couldn't solve it. I knew from that moment I had to." While his classmates watched television, went to the mall, or just hung out with friends, Andrew began studying how geniuses of the past tried to solve the problem.

For a few years he abandoned the problem as he attended high school and college. Eventually he again attacked the problem and this time he was determined to solve it. Finally in 1993, after seven years of intense work, he got it! He estimated he spent over 15,000 hours working on the theorem. His efforts got him named one of *People* magazine's 25 Most Intriguing People of the Year, alongside Oprah Winfrey and Princess Diana. Even today, Wiles doesn't believe that he is that much smarter than other mathematicians. He feels that he was successful solving the problem because he stuck with it longer than others had. He echoes the famous quote by Thomas Edison who said, "Many of life's failures are people who did not realize how close they were to success when they gave up."

QUICK STARTERS

FOUR FAMOUS AUTHORS' SUCCESS STORIES

Choosing a career as a writer can be very frustrating. Thousands of hopeful writers, poets, and authors receive rejections letters every day. They submit mountains of manuscripts to major publishers, only to get turned down, again. Practically all famous writers will tell you about the numerous struggles and disappointments they encountered. They had to be persistent, tough-skinned, and, at times, lucky. Following are four mini-stories of well-known authors who hung in there, and eventually made it.

Margaret Mitchell

She worked as a journalist in Atlanta and had no interest in writing fiction. One day she was thrown from her horse and had to spend many months at home recuperating. After several days of boredom she began writing a romantic novel about Atlanta and the Civil War. It took her almost ten years to finish the book and decided to call it, *Gone with the Wind* which was published in 1936. The book, and the movie, have become classics.

Alex Haley

When Alex was young he started writing adventure stories out of boredom. He found he had a gift— writing. While in the service he was so talented with the pen that he composed love letters for his fellow sailors who sent them to girlfriends and wives. Soon he started submitting articles for publication to magazines. Over the next 8 years he received numerous rejections. He didn't quit and finally produced, *The Autobiography of Malcolm X*. In 1979 he wrote one of the most famous books ever, Roots, which turned into a television mini-series.

J.K. Rowling

J.K. Rowling, the author of the *Harry Potter* books is one of the richest women in the world today. In fact, she is richer than the Queen of England. But she started out very poor. After a difficult divorce in 1993, she and her daughter Jessica moved to Edinburgh, Scotland where they lived in a small, poorly-furnished apartment. While unemployed and receiving state benefits she would spend hours in cafes. While her daughter slept in her carriage, Rowling began writing her first *Harry Potter* book.

Jack Canfield

Have you visited a bookstore lately? If you have, you'll notice that there are numerous versions of *Chicken Soup for the Soul* on the shelf. When Canfield put together the first volume he went to over thirty publishers who turned him down saying, "People aren't interested in reading corny, warm-fuzzy, short stories!" You know the rest of the story.

Career
QUICK STARTERS

LOUISA MAY ALCOTT'S ADVICE FOR PROMISING YOUNG AUTHORS

Many successful people in all professions feel obligated to help young people as they pursue similar careers. The American author, Louisa May Alcott, who wrote *Little Women*, received a letter from a young woman seeking her advice in 1878. Alcott was kind enough to write back and here are a few highlights from her correspondence. Her words are adapted from the book, *The World's Greatest Letters*, by Michele Lovric.

"I can only say to you as I do the many young writers who ask for advice. There is no easy road to successful authorship; it has to be earned by long and patient labor, many disappointments, uncertainties, and trials. Success is often a lucky accident, coming to those who may not deserve it, while others who do have to wait and hope until they earned it."

"I worked for twenty years poorly paid, little known, and quite without any ambition but to eke out a living."

"When I wrote *Hospital Sketches* by the beds of my soldier boys in the shape of letters home I had no idea that I was taking the first step toward what is called fame. It nearly cost my life."

"I hope you will win this joy of writing at least, and I think you will, for you seem to have got on well so far."

"With best wishes for a prosperous and happy New Year. I am your friend: L. M. A.

Courage
QUIPS

Courage
QUIPS

■ The importance of courage

Sir Winston Churchill said, "Courage is the first of the human qualities because it is the quality which guarantees all the others." Think about it!

■ The famous movie cowboy

One of the great old-time movie cowboys, John Wayne once told us, "Courage is being scared to death and saddling up anyway."

■ What are we afraid of?

The Discovery Health Channel polled 1,000 adults. Here were their top five fears: snakes, being buried alive, heights, being bound/tied up, drowning.

■ More fears

A Gallup Poll asked people about their fears. Following are the results:
>   1) snakes
>   2) public speaking
>   3) heights
>   4) being closed in small spaces
>   5) spiders & insects
>   6) needles & getting shots
>   7) mice
>   8) flying in a plane

Courage
QUIPS

■ Do you really need to go?

In his book, *Desert Solitaire*, Edward Abbey tells of visiting a campground bathroom in Utah many years ago. The following sign was posted on the door of the bathroom:

Attention: Watch out for rattlesnakes, coral snakes, whip snakes, vinegaroons, centipedes, millipedes, ticks, mites, black widows, cone-nosed kissing bugs, solpugids, tarantulas, horned toads, Gila monsters, red ants, fire ants, Jerusalem crickets, chinch bugs, and Giant Hairy Desert Scorpions before being seated.

■ The courage to give

The great theologian, Charles Spurgeon reminds us, "To get, we must give; to accumulate, we must scatter; to be happy, we must make others happy; to be spiritually vigorous, we must seek the spiritual good of others. By watering others, we are watered."

■ What is courage?

According to *Webster's New Dictionary*, courage is, "The quality that enables people to meet dangers without giving way to fear."

Courage
QUOTES

Courage
QUOTES

"He who is not courageous enough to take risks will accomplish nothing in life."
-Muhammad Ali

☞**PRIMING THE PUMP:** Think of one risk you took that helped you accomplish something positive in your life. How did you feel? What emotions did you experience as you took that risk? Think of a famous person who took risks on his or her way to success. What challenges did he or she face and what achievements were accomplished?

"I am not afraid of too many things and I got that invincible kind of attitude from my father."
-Queen Latifah

☞**PRIMING THE PUMP:** Who is one adult in your life that gives you the encouragement to take risks? How does he or she assist and/or motivate you? What are some things you say or do for others that encourage them to take positive risks? If you take a risk and it fails, who do you turn to for support? What qualities does that person posses that helps you "get up and try again?"

"Courage is contagious. When a brave man takes a stand, the spines of others are stiffened."
-Billy Graham

☞**PRIMING THE PUMP:** What do you think Billy Graham means when he says "courage is contagious?" When you are taking a stand on something you believe in, how important is it to have others take a stand with you? Explain your response. Have you ever taken a stand or a risk and no one else had the courage to join you? How did you feel? Was there ever a time you didn't have the courage to take a stand or speak up and then later regretted it? Explain what happened and how you felt. What are some possible reasons young people are hesitant to take a stand against things they think are unfair in school?

Courage

QUOTES

"Courage is what it takes to stand up and speak; courage is also what it takes to sit down and listen."

-Sir Winston Churchill

☞**PRIMING THE PUMP:** Can you think of a time when you desired to express your concerns with a teacher or parent but realized, at that time, it was best to remain quiet? What strategies to you use that help you to "bite your tongue" when you really want to say something? Have you ever said something in haste, and then later on regretted it? What happened? Knowing when to speak and when to remain quiet is sometimes called "timing." How can you tell when it is a good time to ask your parents for a favor? How can you tell when it is not a good time to share your concerns with your teacher?

"To sin by silence when they should protest, makes cowards of human beings."

-Abraham Lincoln

☞**PRIMING THE PUMP:** Can you think of a time you remained quiet; you wanted to say something but didn't, and later on felt bad about it? What kept you from speaking up? How might our world be different today if people like Rosa Parks, Martin Luther King, Jr., and Gandhi failed to speak out about injustices? Are there still places in the world today where citizens are afraid to speak out? What prevents them from speaking out against their leaders and their government?

"He who is present at a wrongdoing and does not lift a hand to prevent it, is just as guilty as the wrongdoer."

-Omaha

☞**PRIMING THE PUMP:** When you witness another student being teased or bullied, what do you do? When you witness a peer stealing or vandalizing, does it take courage to report it? What keeps some students from "ratting" on their friends? Have you ever "lost" a friend because you had to tell on him or her? How did that affect you? What would you do if you witnessed someone abusing an animal?

Courage
QUOTES

"You have enemies? Good, that means you stood up for something sometime in your life."

-Sir Winston Churchill

☞**PRIMING THE PUMP:** Can you think of one person in the world today that everyone loves and agrees with? Is there such a person out there? Was there a time you spoke out and/or took a stand on something, knowing you were going to lose a friend or two? What happened? Did Abraham Lincoln have enemies? Who were his enemies? When you are in total disagreement with a stand one of your friends takes, do you ignore him, or try to understand his reasons for taking such a stand? What strategies or interventions do you implement in order to better understand your friend's perspectives?

"The courage to be the real you means you have to own not only the equipment you were born with, but the circumstances of your life as well. Life throws everybody a lot of curves, but those circumstances become part of who you are, where you're coming from, and what you know about. They are part of the unique definition of you."

-Gretchen Cryer

☞**PRIMING THE PUMP:** What does it mean to be the "real you?" What are some possible reasons why living in poverty often takes more courage that living in wealth? Who is someone you know who was born with a severe handicap but displays more courage and determination than most "healthy" people? What do you admire about that person? Do you think people are born with the trait of courage or is it learned? Explain your response.

Courage
QUOTES

"The ultimate measure of a man is not where he stands in moments of comfort, but where he stands at times of controversy."

-Martin Luther King, Jr.

☞**PRIMING THE PUMP:** What are a few controversial topics in which many people lack the courage to truly speak their minds? In which settings or environments do you feel most comfortable to discuss controversial issues? Do you have more respect for those who have the courage to speak out than for those who never express their true feelings? Explain your reasons.

"It takes as much courage to have tried and failed as it does to have tried and succeeded."

-Anne Morrow Lindbergh

☞**PRIMING THE PUMP:** Do you agree or disagree with this quote? Explain your response. Think of a time you displayed courage and achieved your goal. How did you react; what emotions did you feel? Now think of a time you displayed much courage but failed to achieve your goal. How did you react; what emotions did you feel? Does a setback discourage you or motivate you to try harder the next time? How do you encourage your friends to get over their failures and move on?

"Courage doesn't always roar. Sometimes courage is the little voice at the end of the day that says, I'll try again tomorrow."

-Mary Anne Radmacher

☞**PRIMING THE PUMP:** Can quiet, shy, soft-spoken people have just as much, if not more, courage than loud, boisterous people? Think of at least one courageous famous individual who was known for being on the quiet side and list some reasons for his or her success. Do you use positive self-talk at the start of each day and/or at the end of each day to help motivate yourself? What kinds of things do you say to yourself?

Courage
QUICK STARTERS

- *The Courageous Schoolmistress*
- *Courage Stones*
- *Two Kinds of Courage*

THE COURAGEOUS SCHOOLMISTRESS

In her 1965 book, *The Quiet Rebels*, author Margaret Bacon tells the story of a remarkable young lady named Prudence Crandall. Prudence was a young Quaker schoolmistress teaching in Connecticut in 1833 who decided to admit an African American girl to her all-white girls' school. When the town government officials objected to this step, she resolved that rather than dismiss the African American girl named Sarah Harris, she would dismiss all the white girls. Prudence then posted advertisements in newspapers recruiting African American girls for her school. This angered the townspeople who threw garbage at her house, shouted obscenities at her, broke her windows, and drove her away from church. They finally managed to persuade the Connecticut legislature to pass a law against a school "for the education of colored persons who are not inhabitants of the state."

Prudence Crandall was found guilty, and though an appeal was sought for her, it became impossible for her to continue to conduct her school in the face of the inflexible history of the town. The story does have a happy ending. Many years later the state of Connecticut voted Prudence a life pension, removed her arrest report, and apologized for the cruel outrages inflicted upon her.

COURAGE STONES

Many years ago while studying the customs of early Native Americans I came across a unique plan they implemented to help pass on courage to those in need. Their plan involved the use of "courage stones." I took their idea and plugged it into a modern day situation that illustrates the usage of the courage stones.

Emma has to enter the hospital for a serious, life-threatening operation. She is terrified. Her close friend Maddie invites her and several friends to the park a few days before the operation. Emma was told to bring a smooth stone. Maddie, Emma, and four other people sit in a circle. Emma passes her stone to Maddie who rubs it while telling group members of a time she needed courage to handle a difficult situation. Maddie then passes the stone on to another group member who also shares a story of a time she needed courage. Each group member tells a story of courage while holding, rubbing the stone. The stone returns to Emma. She is told to hold on to the stone as much as possible, right up to the time of her operation. Her closest friend keeps the stone while she is being operated on. After the operation, Maddie returns her stone. Emma keeps it as a reminder of the importance of courage.

TWO KINDS OF COURAGE

During World War II Hitler's armies invaded Russia. Although the battles took place on Russian grounds, the Soviet soldiers were often outnumbered by the huge German armies. Hundreds of thousands of Soviet soldiers died from bombs, gun shots, grenades, starvation, and from freezing to death. A young Russian soldier knew that once he entered the army he would probably never see his family and loved ones again.

Many young, frightened soldiers had to make a tough decision. Do they go into battle knowing they wouldn't survive, or do they come up with clever ways of getting discharged so they could return home? Some of these young men would actually shoot themselves in the left hand, hoping they would get discharged. Since almost all soldiers were right-handed, they were willing to lose the use of their left hands in order to avoid fighting on the front lines of battle. Soviet commanders eventually caught on to this trick and the soldiers who continued to shoot themselves in the left hand were labeled as deserters and executed.

What a tough decision these men encountered. Did it take more courage to battle the German soldiers, knowing they would die, or to shoot themselves in the hand?

Creativity & Problem Solving QUIPS

Creativity & Problem Solving
QUIPS

■ Eureka!

Psychologist Paul Paulus at the University of Texas at Arlington's Group Creativity Lab has been researching the art of brainstorming for fifteen years. He has found that group brainstorming really doesn't work very well. In fact, business leaders are "almost always better off" instructing employees to brainstorm individually. Group brainstorming is good team-building, but some of the best ideas come to individuals who eventually shout, "Eureka! I've got a great idea."

■ Yahtzee!

Did you know that the popular board game Yahtzee was created on a yacht by a Canadian couple who wanted something to do when friends came aboard? The game name Yahtzee was derived from the word "yacht."

■ Creative & thankful gold miners

There was a gold-mining town in Alaska. It got its name from the prospectors who came there. There were many ptarmigans (chicken-like birds) that they killed for food. The miners were so thankful to the birds for helping them survive the frigid winters that they wanted to name the town "Ptarmigan." Since none of the men could spell ptarmigan, they named the town after a bird they could spell, Chicken.

■ Changing milk into butter

Hardy travelers along the Oregon Trail in 1843 had to endure bumpy rides across the prairie in their chuck-wagons. The clever travelers found one advantage of the bumpy rides. They discovered that milk could be churned into butter while traveling. They would place a churn of cream on the back of the wagon, and the "bouncing" would turn it into butter.

■ Thanks for the compliment!

If anyone ever calls you a "bird brain," reply by saying, "Thanks for the compliment." Birds are very intelligent, especially crows. These clever birds have been observed placing shelled nuts, clams, and tough-skinned squirrels on roadways, and then let automobiles run over them, thus "opening" their food.

Creativity & Problem Solving
QUIPS

■ Cute, clever, creative coffee shops

A few years I ago my son and I traveled throughout the state of Montana and we were amazed at how many coffee shops we saw. There were so many that the owners had to create clever, attention-getting, names to attract customers. Here are a few of my favorite ones: The Brewed Awakening, Insomniac Expresso, Grizzly Bean, Higher Ground, Pony Expresso, Mountain Mocha, Frisky Beans, Native Grounds, and Java Junction.

■ Clever marksmen

According to the Bible, David was Israel's most famous king. At one time he put together an elite group of warriors known as "David's Thirty." David was very selective in choosing his men. Almost every one of his "thirty" was chosen because of his creative ability to use the bow and arrow and slingshot. They had mastered the skill of handling their weapons either left-or right-handed. Today, many young people know that if they want in future in basketball they must be able to dribble and shoot both left- and right-handed.

■ A creative strategy for learning how to read

James Curry was a slave in North Carolina in the early 1800's. At that time slaves were not allowed to read, but James was determined to do so, even though he knew he would be severely punished if caught with a book in his possession. How did he learn? He got very creative. In the book, *Self-Taught*, Heather Andrea Williams quotes James Curry from his narrative, "When my master's family were all gone away on the Sabbath, I used to go into the house and get down the great Bible, and lie down on the piazza, and read, taking care, however, to put it back before they returned."

■ A faster bicycle

When Soichire Honda was asked how he came up with the idea for inventing a motorcycle he was quoted as saying, "I happened on the idea of fitting an engine to a bicycle simply because I did not want to ride crowded trains and buses."

Creativity & Problem Solving
QUIPS

■ Disgusting, but successful

Every day after school, sixteen year-old Claire had to walk by a construction site where men would whistle at her and make rude comments. One day she shared her concerns with her uncle. He told her of a foolproof way to get the men to stop hassling her. He said, "Pick your nose." It worked.

■ Cool to do drugs?

Thanks to the keen eye of an elementary student, a "mixed" message was halted in New York. He noticed something bizarre as he sharpened the free anti-drug pencil that he and hundreds of other students received at their school. The printing on the pencil read, "Too Cool to Do Drugs." It started out okay, but got worse and worse when the kids started using the pencils. As the pencils were worn down and sharpened, the message changed to: "Cool to Do Drugs." Then: "Do Drugs." The boy was awarded a gift from the pencil company as a thank you for preventing even more possible problems and "mixed" messages.

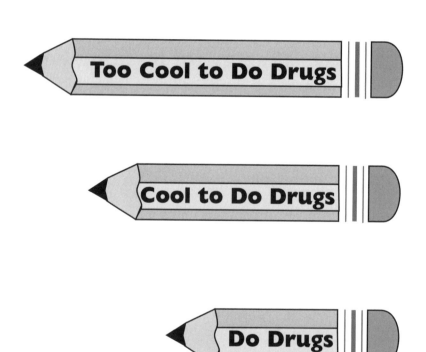

Creativity & Problem Solving
QUOTES

"Shakespeare, Leonardo Da Vinci, Benjamin Franklin, and Lincoln never saw a movie, heard a radio or looked at a television. They had loneliness and knew what to do with it. They were not afraid of being lonely because they knew that was when the creative mood in them would work."

-Carl Sagan

☞**PRIMING THE PUMP:** Do you think it was easier for these famous men to find time to get creative because there were less distractions back then (e.g., television, phones, radio, etc)? Where do you go when you want to be creative? Think of several ways why being alone enhances creativity. Many famous authors do their best writing after midnight; what time of day are you most creative?

"Solitude is as necessary for our creative spirits to develop and flourish as are sleep and food for our bodies to survive."

-Sarah Ban Breathnach

☞**PRIMING THE PUMP:** Obviously sleep and food are needed to assist our creative spirits, but can you think of a couple reasons why solitude is a necessity? Can you think of a few food items that can enhance creativity? What are some food items that negatively affect one's creativity? How can a lack of sleep hurt one's ability to be creative? If you were planning a quiet afternoon alone in the park to be creative, what would you pack in your lunch bag?

"Being bored is an insult to oneself."

-Jules Renard

☞**PRIMING THE PUMP:** How frequently do you hear some of your friends say, "I'm bored?" Have you ever said it? If a young person is bored, whose responsibility is it to relieve the boredom and why? What are some activities that you engage in when the "boredom bug" bites? Jules Renard notes that "being bored is an insult to oneself." What do you think he means by that? Ask your grandparents if they were ever bored when they were children and ask them what activities kept them busy and creative.

Creativity & Problem Solving
QUOTES

"I think, at a child's birth, if a mother could ask a fairy godmother to endow it with the most useful gift, that gift would be curiosity."

-Eleanor Roosevelt

☞**PRIMING THE PUMP:** Can you think of a couple reasons why curiosity can be such a valuable trait? How can curiosity lead to creativity? Can you think of a time that your curiosity got you in trouble? Can you think of an object, machine, or some gadget that you took apart just to see how it worked? Often parents will tell a child "not to" look in a room or in a drawer. When a parent says that, does it make the child even more curious? What is the greatest discovery that your curiosity helped you find?

"Millions of persons long for immortality who do not know what to do with themselves on a rainy afternoon."

-Susan Ertz

☞**PRIMING THE PUMP:** When you are sitting at home on a rainy afternoon, what kinds of careers are you thinking about and where would you like to live when you grow up? Instead of just sitting and thinking, what are some things you could be doing that would enhance your chances of achieving future goals? Many people love to read on rainy days. What activities to you especially enjoy on rainy days? Do you think famous athletes like Tiger Woods, Lance Armstrong, and Annika Sorenstam cancel their outdoor practices when it's raining? Think of a few reasons why they need to practice in the rain.

Creativity & Problem Solving QUOTES

"I 'must do something' always solves more problems than 'something must be done.'"

-anonymous

☞**PRIMING THE PUMP:** Can you think of a time when several people sat around and complained about something but no one did anything about it? How did you feel? What finally happened? When you see litter along the road in your neighborhood, do you ignore it, complain about it or pick it up? If you are concerned about graffiti in the bathrooms at school, instead of complaining about the problem, what action could you take? What would you say to a person who always seems to be upset with the president, but he or she never votes? Do you have a success story about a group of people who worked together to solve a major problem at school or in the community? Can you think of a famous person who wasn't afraid to take a stand (alone) to confront a serious problem or injustice?

"Most people spend more time and energy going around problems than in trying to solve them."

-Henry Ford

☞**PRIMING THE PUMP:** Horace had an extreme fear of the dentist. To address this problem he refused to go for check-ups. The longer he went between visits, the more cavities he got and visits were more painful to him. If he would have stuck to his two regular visits a year for preventive measures, he would have had fewer "tooth" problems and less painful visits. Horace was doing exactly what Henry Ford said, spending more time and energy going around the dentist problem than trying to resolve it. Have you been guilty of "going around problems?" Give an example. How can attacking problems "head on" and immediately, help eliminate some of the stress and worries in your life? How often have you heard teachers and parents tell you and others, "Don't put off until tomorrow what you can do today?" Why do you think adults preach that message?

Creativity & Problem Solving
QUOTES

"It's not that I'm so smart, it's just that I stay with problems longer."

-Albert Einstein

☞**PRIMING THE PUMP:** Some people have a very low frustration level; they tend to quit or give up quickly when addressing problems. Others have "bulldog tenacity," they won't quick until the problem is resolved. What is your approach to addressing problems? Can you think of a famous athlete, scientist, inventor, or political figure that became famous because he or she refused to quit or give up? Why is the world a better place because of this person's "tenacity?"

"Hot heads and cold hearts never solved anything."

-Billy Graham

☞**PRIMING THE PUMP:** What does Billy Graham mean by "hot head?" What is a "cold heart?" What are the possible serious consequences of trying to solve a problem when you are angry? What are the possible serious consequences of trying to solve a problem without compassion for others? Can you think of some advantages of seeking solitude before trying to solve important issues that affect your life and others?

Creativity & Problem Solving QUOTES

"If I have eight hours to chop a tree, I will spend six hours sharpening my axe."
-Abraham Lincoln

☞**PRIMING THE PUMP:** Many people attempt to solve a problem without doing their homework. What might happen to a person who attempts to climb Mt. Everest without first learning about breathing problems at higher altitudes, temperature changes, slippery conditions, and proper nutrition? Should a runner, who has never run more than a mile, show up at the starting line of the New York Marathon? Can you think of a situation when you took time to prepare, did your homework, and practiced (role played) before tackling a problem? What happened? Did you ever fail at something because you didn't take time to prepare? What happened? If Abe Lincoln and others were given an axe and eight hours to chop down the tree, do you think he might finish before the others because he took more time to prepare?

"One cannot manage too many affairs. Like pumpkins in the water, one pops up while you try to hold down the others."
-Chinese proverb

☞**PRIMING THE PUMP:** Have you ever felt overwhelmed with having so many problems? How do you handle the stress when this happens? Do you try to solve every problem on your own or do you seek help? Who are some people that you can turn to for help and advice?

Q 101

Creativity & Problem Solving
QUICK STARTERS

- The House of Chicken Feathers
- Anagrams Enhance Creativity
- The Bus Driver and the Shepherd Boys
- Magpie Hats
- A Clever Coyote Catcher

THE HOUSE OF CHICKEN FEATHERS

One of the world's most famous humanitarians, Albert Schweitzer said, "Even if it's a little thing, do something for those who have need of help, something for which you get no pay but the privilege of doing it." Helping others is important, but it isn't always simple or easy. A kind missionary in Peking, China a hundred and fifty years ago encountered numerous problems when he showed kindness to the poor. It would have been easy for him to give up. Instead, he got very creative and his efforts paid off.

Harland Sinclair left his home in London and traveled to China to serve as a missionary. When he traveled throughout Peking he was shocked to see so many poor and homeless people sleeping in the streets at night. He set a personal goal to do all he could to help the poor have a safe, warm place to spend their evenings.

Harland eventually found an old abandoned warehouse that he was granted permission to use for his plan. He covered the dirt floor with a thick layer of chicken feathers. Every night the poor arrived by the hundreds, adults and children. The missionary charged visitors a penny and each one was given a blanket to borrow for the night. After a few days a major problem occurred. Many of the poor failed to leave their borrowed blankets behind. Obviously Harland was upset with his blankets being stolen but he wished to continue his mission of helping the homeless. He had to get creative.

Along with the help of the local Chinese government, a new strategy was developed. A huge felt blanket was suspended from the ceiling by a system of cables. When the poor arrived each night and were settled in, a bell rang and then pulleys slowly lowered the massive blanket down over the poor and the chicken feathers. Holes were cut into the blankets so the people could stick their heads out and breathe. At seven o'clock in the morning the bell rang again and the pulleys lifted the blanket off the sleepers. Hundreds of poor headed back to streets after a good night's rest.

Harland's persistence and creativity paid off. He left China with a good feeling knowing that his work had a positive impact on helping the needy.

ANAGRAMS ENHANCE CREATIVITY

Word puzzles, Sudoku, Kakuro, crossword puzzles and other pad and pencil activities are not only fun and challenging, but they also enhance one's creativity. One of the best word activities to build one's ability to become more creative focuses on anagrams. What are anagrams? An anagram is a word or phrase formed by rearranging the letters of another word or phrase. Following are a few examples.

> *Clint Eastwood......................Old West Action*
>
> *Elvis.................................Lives*
>
> *Dormitory...........................Dirty room*
>
> *Listen...............................Silent*
>
> *The eyes...........................They see*
>
> *Butterfly...........................Flutter-by*
>
> *Christmas tree......................Search, set, trim*
>
> *Statue of Liberty...................Built to stay free*
>
> *Astronomers........................Moon starers*
>
> *Tokyo...............................Kyoto*
>
> *Spandex............................Expands*
>
> *Slot machines......................Cash lost in 'em*

People have been "playing" with anagrams for centuries. Thirteenth century Jewish mystics, called cabalists, thought that by reciting letters from the Hebrew alphabet in different orders could create miracles. In the early seventeenth century, King Louis XIII appointed a Royal Anagramist at a fabulous salary. An English speaking anagramist is someone who, if asked to name the four points of a compass replies, "Thorn, Shout, Seat, Stew." Lewis Carroll (1832-1898), who authored the book, *Alice in Wonderland*, enjoyed playing and making up word games. He once coined an anagram for the then British Prime Minister, William Ewart Gladstone. Shuffling the letters spelling that name he changed them to read, Wild Agitator—Means Well.

Get creative with anagrams. Shuffle the letters to your name, your friends, famous people, singers, athletes, politicians, and common phrases. See what you can do.

THE BUS DRIVER AND THE SHEPHERD BOYS

Notes from the Hyena's Belly is a remarkable book written by Nega Mezlekia in which he tells of his boyhood growing up in war-torn Ethiopia. Scattered throughout the book are numerous stories how he and others had to be resilient and creative in order to survive famine, war, and attacks by wild animals. One of the most fascinating stories involves a bus driver who had to drive his old bus up and down narrow roads on a steep mountain. Not only did the driver have to navigate treacherous roads, he had to deal with young shepherd boys who would hide and hurl rocks at the bus with their sling-shots.

The bus driver told Nega about his struggles with the boys and how he eventually resolved the problem. The driver invited Nega to ride the bus with him and to observe his creative intervention with the shepherd boys. As the bus slowly crawled up a muddy, narrow mountain trail the driver told Nega about the young lads they were soon to encounter. He noted, "In the beginning I would get very angry at the rock-throwers and I would run after them. I wanted them arrested, but they only laughed and I couldn't catch them. I soon realized that these boys were poor, lonely, and had little excitement in their lives. My travels up the hill were one of the few highlights in their lives. They looked forward to running after me with their sling-shots and their barking dogs. They aren't bad kids. They just need a little love and attention. Watch what happens when I spot the boys. They don't throw rocks anymore."

The driver came to stop and a group of boys rushed towards the bus. He reached under his seat and pulled out a duffel bag and stepped out. As the boys circled around he asked them questions about their families, their sheep and goats, and school. He shook their hands, patted them on their backs, and gave them kind words of encouragement. Then he opened his duffle game and gave the boys candy, small toys, paper and pencils, and a couple soccer balls. Before he got back on the bus he asked the boys if there was anything else they needed that he could bring on his next visit. The boys waved good-bye and smiled.

The bus driver told Nega that a few dollars in candy and toys costs him less than having to constantly replace broken windows on the bus. By showing a bit of kindness and compassion, instead of anger and revenge, he was able to build a positive relationship with the shepherd boys. Nega learned a valuable lesson from the kind bus driver.

MAGPIE HATS

There was a big problem in some of the small tourist towns along the northern coasts of Australia. It was mating season for the pesky magpies. These birds can become very aggressive as they protect their nests and eggs. Because the birds were dive-bombing and actually biting people on their heads, few tourists were walking the beach or spending money in restaurants or gifts shops. The attacking magpies were causing the small towns a lot of money. Thanks to the creative mind of a young boy named Steve, one small town successfully resolved many of the magpie problems.

Young Steve often walked the beaches and studied nature. He especially enjoyed the gulls, shore birds, and magpies. Several times he had been attacked by the magpies and he often overheard merchants complaining about how the birds were hurting business. Many shop owners met to brainstorm strategies to address the problem. Steve attended the meetings and wished he could help. He understood why the people wanted the birds to leave but he didn't like hearing suggestions about shooting them.

Because Steve loved animals and nature, he was constantly reading books on those topics. One day while he sat and observed the dive-bombing magpies he remembered a book he recently read about men who were building railroads in the jungles of Africa in the late 1800's. It was a dangerous job as several men died from snakebites and attacks by lions. Most of the men who died from lion attacks were the slaves from India known as coolies. The more the coolies were attacked, the more they began to uncover a fascinating fact. They discovered that lions would never attack a human that was looking at them. If lions could see a human's eyes, it wouldn't attack. Soon, coolies starting making masks to put on the back of their heads. The masks highlighted a large set of eyes. Coolies who wore the masks were never attacked from behind.

Steve got an idea. He started making hats with drawings of people's faces on the top. He made sure the masks had a large set of eyes on them. He sat up a booth on the beach and sold his magpie protection hats for $5.00 each. Many beach walkers returned and purchased hats. Almost all the magpies stopped their attacks and business owners were happy to see tourists return.

Steve not only helped the business owners and tourists, he made a nice profit thanks to his ingenuity. Have you ever thought of creative ways to help others and make a little money?

A CLEVER COYOTE CATCHER

One of the craftiest, wisest, smartest animals is the coyote. Coyotes are also one of the most curious. Author Dorothy Parker wrote, "The cure for boredom is curiosity; there is no cure for curiosity." Coyotes are never bored! Although many people admire the coyote, most farmers in the west see them as an enemy because they attack and kill chickens, small livestock, and even the family pet cat. Over the years millions of these predators have been trapped and shot by frustrated farmers. Often these canines become so clever that they outsmart the hunters. They have been known to spring traps without getting caught and they have found unique ways to tunnel underground to get into chicken coops.

In his book, *The Voice of the Coyote*, J. Frank Dobie tells the tale of one coyote that killed hundreds of chickens and was so clever that it couldn't be captured. Hunters and farmers tried numerous tricks to catch the sly coyote with no success. Following are a few of the trap tricks that didn't work:

- **Tie a live chicken to the trap.**
- **Sprinkle coyote urine on the trap.**
- **Sprinkle lady's perfume on the trap.**
- **Leave a trail of meat that ends at a set trap.**
- **Cover the trap with leaves and then place deer ears on top.**

These and numerous other tricks could not capture this creative, curious coyote. Then things got worse. The coyote started killing sheep. Something had to be done. The best "coyote catcher" in the country was contacted. When he arrived he told the farmers that the best way to capture a coyote is to focus on its sense of curiosity. When he told the farmers that he could catch the coyote with an alarm clock, they laughed. J. Frank Dobie tells the story, "The sheep-killing coyote carefully avoided every trick until one day the famous coyote catcher wound up an ordinary alarm clock, put it in a tin can, and buried the can with a sprinkling of dirt over the lid along one of the ways the coyote was using. A trap was buried adjacent to the clock so that if the coyote investigated he would almost have to step into it. Hearing the ticking in the ground was too much for this coyote. Curiosity about something that was none of his business made him negligent of what had become the main business of his life aside from eating." The coyote got trapped!

Another problem solved, thanks to one person's creativity. As the saying goes, "Sometimes you've got to outsmart the fox," or in this case, the coyote.

Q 107

Getting Along With Others

QUIPS

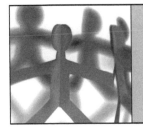

Getting Along With Others
QUIPS

■ Sit down

When you and another person have a conflict, remember the Native American saying, "Standing is confrontation, sitting is conversation."

■ Which one are you!

Newspaper columnist and advice-giver, Abigail Van Buren said, "There are two kinds of people in the world; those who walk into a room and say, 'There you are!' and those who say, 'Here I am!'"

■ It's how you say it

It's not so much what you say,
as the manner in which you say it.
It's not so much the language you use,
as the tone in which you convey it.

-anonymous

■ Share the burden

Good advice: *Trouble shared is troubled halved.*

■ Stamford or Ayrshire?

Here is a unique way one town resolved a conflict. Stamford is a big city in Connecticut. This is how the city got its name. Some early settlers wanted to name the town Stamford, while others preferred Ayrshire. Since the people couldn't agree, they had two roosters fight. One rooster was given the name Stamford and the other was named Ayrshire. The people agreed that the town would be named after the winning rooster. Stamford won!

■ Incomplete pass

Many angry people are full of hurt and pain. Often they try to pass on their pain to others who, in turn, pass the pain on to others, and so on. When someone tries to pass their pain to you, drop it like an incomplete pass in football. Just because someone is unkind to you, is it "ok" for you turn around and be mean to someone else?

Q
109

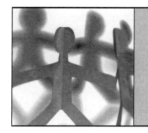

Getting Along With Others
QUIPS

■ Wherever or whenever?

Writer Oscar Wilde had an interesting thought when he stated, "Some cause happiness **wherever** they go, others **whenever** they go." Think about it!

■ Constructive conflict

"Conflict can be constructive if we are hard on issues and soft on people. We tend to be hard on both or soft on both but not good at separating the two." –anonymous

■ Strange but true

Eugene Schneider of Carteret, New Jersey was sued for divorce by his wife in 1976. The court ordered Eugene to divide his property equally between his wife and himself. He took the judgment literally, got out his chain saw, and cut the couple's home in two!

■ Trouble getting along with his fans

Former rock singer Carl Perkins's most popular song was Blue Suede Shoes. Late in his career, he put on blue suede shoes for all of his concerts. He wore the showy shoes with dread because after the performance fans would mob the stage to step on his blue suede shoes, exactly as the song urged them not to do.

■ Learn to love them

Occasionally we may meet someone that we just can't get along with. Maybe we need to take the advice given by the Department of Agriculture who received a letter from a frustrated gardener seeking advice for dealing with weeds. The department responded, "We have no more advice on how to rid your garden of weeds. We suggest, therefore, that you learn to love them."

■ Be patient

Developing a positive relationship with a difficult person will be a marathon, not a 100-yard dash. It will take time—be patient.

Getting Along With Others
QUOTES

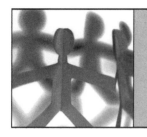

Getting Along With Others
QUOTES

"The most important single ingredient in the formula of success is knowing how to get along with people."

-Theodore Roosevelt

☞**PRIMING THE PUMP:** Explain how having the gift of 'getting along with others' might get you farther in life than your academic achievements. What are some things you are presently doing, besides schoolwork, that are helping you improve relationships with others? Think of a job you would like to have later in life, and then list several reasons why 'getting along with others' will be crucial to your success.

"Misunderstandings don't exist; only the failure to communicate."

-Senegalese proverb

☞**PRIMING THE PUMP:** Have you ever been 'misunderstood?' What happened and how did you feel? Have you ever 'misunderstood' someone else? How did you and that person resolve the misunderstanding? What are a few communication skills that you and your friends need in order to resolve misunderstandings? Explain the importance of being a good listener.

"Friend: One who knows all about you and loves you just the same."

-Elbert Hubbard

☞**PRIMING THE PUMP:** What is your description of a true friend? What are some things you might discuss with your best friend that you wouldn't discuss with family members? What are some things your friends say or do that make you feel comfortable around them? Have you ever gone through a period of time when you felt you didn't have a true friend? How did you cope during that difficult period?

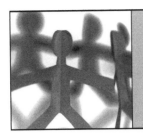

Getting Along With Others
QUOTES

"When you choose your friends, don't be shortchanged by choosing personality over character."

W. Somersett Maugham

☞**PRIMING THE PUMP:** How important is one's character when you are choosing friends? How long does it take to discover one's true character? Have you ever been "fooled" by a friend's hidden, negative character traits? How did you handle it? Why do you think so many young people choose friends based on looks, personality, and 'how they dress' instead of seeking friends with positive character traits?

"In an encounter with a difficult person, always assume, at least initially, that the person is trying to do the best he or she can and that there is a redeeming explanation for the difficult behavior."

-Mark. I. Rosen

☞**PRIMING THE PUMP:** Do you think all difficult people really mean to be difficult? Explain. What are some events that could be going on in one's life that may cause him or her to be hard to get along with? Has anyone ever told you that were we a difficult person? How did you react? Describe a time you were angry with a difficult person, and how your feelings changed once she told you about some struggles she was going through.

"How to argue should not be discussed during an argument."
-Hugh Prather

☞**PRIMING THE PUMP:** Do you think people are open to suggestions about the rules of arguing when they are very emotional? Explain your response. Explain how you feel when, in the midst of a heated argument, the other person questions your techniques. How important is it for you and your friends to agree on certain rules of arguing or discussing "touchy" issues? What are some possible rules that you and your friends may wish to agree upon?

Q 113

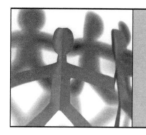

Getting Along With Others
QUOTES

"In real conflict resolution, you stop arguing when you notice it is not working. If you continue to argue, you're looking for drama more than harmony."

-David Richo

☞**PRIMING THE PUMP:** How can you tell when it is time to stop arguing with someone? What are some possible negative consequences that could occur if you and your friend allowed an argument to go on too long? Do you believe that some people actually enjoy arguing? Explain your answer. What are some advantages of resolving conflicts privately, as opposed to being in the presence of peers?

"I never saw an instance of one or two disputants convincing the other by argument."

-Thomas Jefferson

☞**PRIMING THE PUMP:** What are some possible reasons why arguing people are seldom able to convince the other that he or she is wrong? In an argument, do the disputants usually practice good listening skills? In an argument, how can you tell if the other person is really listening to you? Be honest; have you ever seen an argument end with one of the combatants announcing, "Hey, you are right. I'm wrong. I apologize."? If you have, describe what happened?

"Better to be quarreling than to be lonesome."

-Irish proverb

☞**PRIMING THE PUMP:** What are some possible reasons some folks would rather quarrel than be lonesome? Is it possible to go through life without ever quarreling? Explain your answer. What are some possible advantages to getting into an occasional argument? Can people who are truly in love with each other have occasional quarrels/arguments? Is it possible for two people who do not like each other to never quarrel/argue?

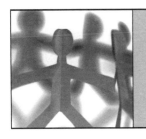

Getting Along With Others
QUOTES

"The greatest conflicts are not between two people but between one person and himself."

-Garth Brooks

☞**PRIMING THE PUMP:** What are some positive reasons for having personal conflicts? What topic or situation causes you to have "arguments" with yourself? When you have personal conflicts, do you ever seek advice from others? Who do you go to and why? How might your health be affected if you continue to have unresolved personal conflicts? Where do you go to be alone in order to work on your personal conflicts?

"People love others not for who they are but for how they make us feel."
-Irwin Federman

☞**PRIMING THE PUMP:** When you are feeling down, who do you turn to that often lifts your spirits? What does this special person say or do that makes you feel better? What personality traits do you possess that make others feel warm and comfortable when they are around you? What behaviors in others keep you from seeking them out when you need a lift?

"There's something wrong if you're always right."
-Arnold H. Glasgow

☞**PRIMING THE PUMP:** Do you know someone who always thinks he or she is right? How do you feel being around that person? Are you able to admit that you are wrong once in a while? How do you feel when you do admit it? How can your opinion change about someone when he admits that he was wrong? How will your relationships with others suffer if your goal is to win every conflict?

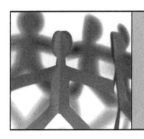

Getting Along With Others
QUOTES

"You can make more friends in two months by becoming more interested in other people than you can in two years by trying to get people interested in you."

-anonymous

☞**PRIMING THE PUMP:** How do you feel being others who are constantly talking about themselves and their accomplishments? Do you prefer being around boastful people, or people who truly seem interested in you? Please explain. How do you feel when a friend or adult seeks you out for help and/or advice? How do you show others that you are interested in what they have to say?

"The way to make a true friend is to be one. Friendship implies loyalty, esteem, cordiality, sympathy, attention, readiness to aid, to help, to stick with, to fight for, if need be. Radiate friendship and it will return sevenfold."

-B.C. Forbes

☞**PRIMING THE PUMP:** What is a "fair weather" friend? B.C. Forbes lists several characteristics of a true friend. Are there other characteristics that you look for in a friend? Can you think of a time one of your best friends let you down? What happened and how did you feel? What was one the greatest sacrifices a friend made for you? How did you show your appreciation?

"I cannot give you the formula for success, but I can give you the formula for failure—try to please everybody."

-Herbert Bayer Swope

☞**PRIMING THE PUMP:** Is it possible to have everybody like you? What are the possible dangers of trying to make everyone like you? Think of at least one well-known person in history who had numerous enemies but was still considered a hero? Who were his or her enemies? Has there ever been a person, present or past, who was loved by everyone? Explain your answer. Describe a situation where you had to take a stand or risk at the expense of losing a friend or two? How did you deal with it?

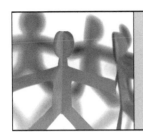

Getting Along With Others
QUOTES

"Happy people are constantly evaluating themselves. Unhappy people are constantly evaluating others."

-William Glasser

☞**PRIMING THE PUMP:** How do you feel when you are around someone who is always talking badly about other people? What strategies or interventions do you attempt to get that negative person to stop bad-mouthing others? Do you tell your friends the things that the negative person was saying about them? Why or why not? Do you have a better chance at changing yourself or changing others? Explain how the behaviors of others around you can change once you change your behavior.

Getting Along With Others
QUICK STARTERS

- *All or Nothing*
- *The Purr and the Snore*

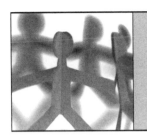

ALL OR NOTHING

Laurie and Michelle were good friends until Michelle opened a can of Coca-Cola that was worth $10,000. Several years ago Laurie stopped by the store to purchase a twelve-pack of Coca-Cola. Later that day her friend Michelle came by for a visit and Laurie offered her a can of soda. When Michelle finished the drink she noticed some printing on the bottom of the can. It read that the can was a grand prize worth $10,000 from a Coca-Cola contest. She jumped for joy as she told Laurie about her winning can. Laurie took the can and claimed that the prize money should be hers because she bought it. Michelle argued that the prize was hers because Laurie gave her the can of soda. Their argument went on for days; they couldn't resolve the conflict. Eventually they broke off their friendship and took the case to court.

According to an article in the USA Today on October 6, 2000 Judge John Clark ended the debate. His decision awarded the $10,000 to Laurie because she was the one who purchased the can. Laurie won the money but lost a good friend. Couldn't they have resolved the conflict without going to court? Was it possible to resolve the conflict and still remain friends?

THE PURR AND THE SNORE

Do you believe everything that people tell you about others? Have you ever, for instance, heard so many negative things about Zoey, that you had an unfair picture of her in your head even before ever meeting her? Then, once you met her, did that negative picture change and you became friends? Have you ever had someone tell you something like, "You won't like Jazmine, she's too bossy," and later on, after meeting her, you didn't notice any bossiness? People try to influence our thoughts about friends, movies, music, and restaurants. I hope you don't let these people influence you too much; you need to find out for yourself. Following is an experiment described in the book, *A Perfumed Scorpion*, by Idries Shah. I hope it helps you learn not to jump to conclusions. You need to be patient and perceptive.

There is an experiment known as the "Cat and Snore." A recording of a cat's purr was played to random collections of people. Those who were told it was a human snore really disliked it, and turned away in disgust. Those who were informed that it was the purr of a contented cat (apart from those who disliked cats) expressed a desire to hear more. When snores were played, in recording, to an audience whose members had been told that they were an amplified recording of a kitten purring, everyone expressed pleasure, except, of course, those who did not like cats.

Gifts, Talents, & Strengths

QUIPS

Gifts, Talents, & Strengths
QUIPS

■ The last words of the great artist Leonardo da Vinci

"I have offended God and mankind because my work did not reach the quality it should have."

■ What are the odds?

Talk about a talented athlete; check this out. In July of 2000, David Howard of Brookings, South Dakota shot a hole-in-one on a golf course and then the next day he rolled a perfect 300-game in bowling. *USA TODAY* sports analysts figured the odds of doing this was 230 million to 1.

■ Peanuts, Charlie Brown, Snoopy, and Lucy

Charles Schulz, the great cartoonist and creator of the Peanuts cartoon strip, was asked once how he felt about his artistic and creative abilities. He responded, "I don't think I'm a true artist. I would love to be like Picasso. But I can draw pretty well and I can write pretty well, and I think I'm doing the best with whatever abilities I've been given."

■ Gifted observers

John Fanshawe and Terry Stevenson saw 342 different bird species on a single day in Kenya— the highest total ever achieved anywhere in the world.

■ Musical instruments & weapons

It's often been said that if you put a musical instrument in a child's hands, early enough, those same hands will never hold a gun, knife, or weapon.

■ The plumber and the sculptor

The following anonymous quote helps us to put things into perspective. "Guido the plumber and Michelangelo obtained their marble from the same quarry, but what each saw in the marble made the difference between a nobleman's sink and a brilliant sculpture."

■ A gifted judge

Samuel Leibowitz was one of the cleverest, most creative judges ever to serve the city of New York. In 1947 he had to confront numerous guilty pickpockets in court. One of the punishments he dished out to these criminals was to make them wear boxing gloves in the street, making it impossible for them to pick the pockets of pedestrians.

Gifts, Talents, & Strengths
QUIPS

■ Be patient

Author Po Bronson believes only a small portion of our gifts and interests have shown themselves by age eighteen.

■ Same about of time, different talents

Motivational speaker Zig Ziglar reminds us, "We all have the same amount of time, but not the same talent and ability. Those who use their time well, however, often surpass those with more ability."

■ It's never too late

Tiger Woods starting playing golf at the age of four. Tennis greats Venus and Serena Williams were winning major tournaments before they were teenagers. Helen Klein didn't start running until she was 55. Now, at the age of 83, she is still running and has completed 78 marathons and 143 ultra-marathons (races longer than 26.2 miles).

■ Your gift + commitment = success

What is your special gift or talent? What would happen if you spent five hours a week for ten years nurturing it? Wow! Amazing things would happen! LeAnn, at the age of eight, starting practicing piano for five hours a week and by the time she was eighteen she had spent a total of 2,600 hours practicing. Do you think she got pretty good at it?

■ If you really want to, you'll find time

Philosopher William Feather said, "We all find time to do what we really want to do."

■ You've got to believe

Billy Mills grew up living in poverty on a Sioux Indian reservation in South Dakota. He became a talented runner who pulled off one of the greatest upsets in history as he won a gold medal in the 10,000 meter race in the 1964 Tokyo Olympics. Here is what he wrote in his training diary prior to the big race. "God has given me the ability, the rest is up to me. Believe. Believe. Believe."

Gifts, Talents, & Strengths
QUOTES

Gifts, Talents, & Strengths
QUOTES

"To give anything less than your best is to sacrifice the gift."
-Steve Prefontaine

☞**PRIMING THE PUMP:** What are one or two special gifts and talents you were blessed with when you were born? What are you presently doing to enrich your gifts? Do you think special gifts will fade away if you don't use them? Name at least one talented person you admire and tell how he or she took advantage of their gifts. What is one gift you wish you had and why?

"A great deal of talent is lost in this world for want of a little courage."
-Sydney Smith

☞**PRIMING THE PUMP:** Explain why one needs courage to make the best of his or her talents. Can you think of a person you know that has talent but never really used it? What is that person's talent and what is keeping him or her from taking advantage of it? What are a few things you could say or do that might help encourage that person? How might our world be a better place to live if more people utilized their special gifts and talents?

"People who are unable to motivate themselves must be content with mediocrity, no matter how impressive their talents."
-Andrew Carnegie

☞**PRIMING THE PUMP:** Do you think people can be truly happy in life if they don't use their talents? Explain your response. Whose responsibility is it to motivate you to use your talents? Who is one person who praised you on your special talent and how did his or her words affect you? Have you ever talked to adults who are now angry with themselves because they didn't practice their talents when they were young? Besides anger, what other emotions might they be feeling?

Q 125

Gifts, Talents, & Strengths
QUOTES

"If you flatter me, I may not believe you. If you ignore me, I won't remember you. If you criticize me, I may not like you. If you encourage me, I won't forget you."

-Chuck Update

☞**PRIMING THE PUMP:** Who are some people in your life that encourage you to build on your talents? Tell how important their kind words are to you. Have you ever had an adult in your life that you really cared about, that was overly critical of you and your talents, or who completely ignored you? How did you feel? What are some things you say or do to encourage others? Ten years from now, are you more likely to remember the candy bar your teacher gave you, or the kind, encouraging words he said you? Explain your answer.

"The real tragedy of life is not being limited to one talent, but in failing to use that one talent."

-Edgar Watson Howe

☞**PRIMING THE PUMP:** Do you believe that some people are born with more gifts and talents than others, or has everyone been given the same amount? Does the number of talents one has determine his or her potential for success? Explain your response. What are some possible negative consequences of spending your time balancing several talents rather than focusing on just one or two? There is a popular saying that goes, "He is a jack of all trades, but master of none." What do you think that means?

"No one has your unique gifts. You possess talents and capabilities that other people, including the ones you admire, can only dream of. And those unique gifts are what you must bring to the world."

-Kevin Nelson

☞**PRIMING THE PUMP:** What are some talents you possess that others have told you they admire? Is it possible that famous people like Michael Jordan, Mia Hamm, or Maya Angelou wished they had one of your gifts or talents? Should people feel some responsibility for bringing their gifts to the world? Explain the importance of people bringing your talents to the world.

Q 126

Gifts, Talents, & Strengths
QUOTES

"Talent is God-given; be thankful. Conceit is self-given, be careful."
-Thomas LaMance

☞**PRIMING THE PUMP:** How do you express your "thanks" for the talents and gifts you've been given? What does it mean to be conceited? How can conceit effect friendships? How do you feel when you encounter people who boast about their talents?

"Ability may get you to the top, but it takes character to keep you there."
-John Wooden

☞**PRIMING THE PUMP:** Explain the importance of combining positive character traits with one's talents. Many people who make it to the top (athletes, musicians, actors) have character lapses; why do you think that happens? What impact does the lack of character in famous people have on children? Years from now, do you want to be remembered more for your talents or for your positive character traits? Please explain your answer.

"I was given the gifts to become not only an athlete but also a businessman, a thinker who could dispel the myth that most athletes are dumb jocks who can't see beyond the next game."
-Magic Johnson

☞**PRIMING THE PUMP:** Think of a few reasons why young people should pursue a good education while they are nurturing their gifts and talents. What do you think will get your farther in life, your talents and gifs or a college degree? Explain your response. What are a few ways you could combine your talents and educational degree into a successful career?

Q 127

Gifts, Talents, & Strengths
QUOTES

"Parents, take interest in your children's interests, or they will lose interest in their interests."

-Amish saying

☞**PRIMING THE PUMP:** How important is it to have an adult show interest in your interests (hobbies, talents, sports, music, art, and others)? What are some ways parents can support and encourage their children? Besides your parents, what other adult has been a great motivator to you? How did that person encourage you? How can you show interest in your parents' interests?

Gifts, Talents, & Strengths
QUICK STARTERS

- *Amber's Gift of Giving to Others*
- *The Talented Free Throw Shooter*

Gifts, Talents, & Strengths
QUICK STARTERS

AMBER'S GIFT OF GIVING TO OTHERS

When we think of people who have special gifts and talents we often think of those who excel in sports, music, art, acting, writing, teaching, science and other high-profile occupations. But there are some people who have the gift of helping others. These people aren't searching for special recognition; they just want to help others—that's their gift or talent. Amber Hoffman is one of those special people.

I learned about Amber many years ago while watching the morning news. As a young child her hero was Mother Teresa. Amber was amazed with her hero's time and energy that was aimed at the needy. At the age of 10 or 11 Amber had read four books about Mother Teresa and she wanted to be just like her.

When Amber rode the school bus home every day, it passed through some of the poorest parts of Baltimore and she would see numerous cold and hungry homeless people. She decided to take action to help these people. She formed a group of young volunteers to meet at her house each Saturday morning to make sandwiches for the homeless. Amber called her group "The Happy Helpers for the Homeless." Soon her group was making 600 sandwiches every weekend. Her mother would drive her to the city so she could pass out the sandwiches to the homeless. Thanks to Mother Teresa, Amber set a goal, got businesses to donate meat and bread, rounded up volunteers, and spent her Saturdays doing something great to help her community.

THE TALENTED FREE THROW SHOOTER*

Harold "Bunny" Levitt loved playing basketball, but he could never make the team because he was only 5'4" tall, he couldn't pass, couldn't dribble, and he couldn't make many lay-ups. The only thing he was good at was making free throws. Even his free throw shooting suffered at times because other players teased him about the way he shot the ball. He would toss the ball underhanded, placing two hands on the ball. Others would laugh and yell out, "You shoot like a girl," or "Why are you shooting granny style?" He wasn't wanted on any team.

One day, Harold saw a poster advertising a basketball free throw shooting contest. For weeks he practiced secretly for the contest. He shot hundreds free throws everyday. He usually practiced early in the morning or in the dark so other boys wouldn't tease or bother him.

Many people questioned him on the day of the contest. One boy said, "What are you doing here? You can't play basketball!" Many people gathered to watch Harold start shooting. As usual, he grabbed the ball with two hands and shot underhanded. Most everyone laughed and pointed at him, but soon the laughing stopped. Harold swished one basket after another. He made 100 in a row, 200 in a row, 300, 400, and then missed his first shot which would have been number 500. Yes, he made 499 in a row!

The contest supervisor told Harold that he was the winner of the contest. Harold would not take the prize. Instead, he returned to the free throw line and started shooting again. Hardly anyone left. People were amazed as he continued to make one shot after another. At 2:30 in the morning, the janitor had to beg him to stop shooting so he could lock-up the gym and go home. When he stopped, he had made another 371 in a row. For the contest he made 870 out of 871 shots! Nobody teased Harold again.

Soon after that, Harold was invited to travel and play with the world famous Harlem Globetrotters. Also, he would travel the country to challenge others in foul shooting contests. He offered $1,000 to anyone who could beat him in a contest of 100 free throws. He never lost. Harold's talent of shooting free throws made him famous!

Adapted from the book Monday Morning Messages by Tom Carr (Youthlightbooks.com)

Goals & Dreams

QUIPS

Goals & Dreams QUIPS

■ The powerful pencil

Do you have a dream? Then write it down. Author and evangelist, Joyce Meyer says, "A #2 pencil and a dream can take you anywhere."

■ No excuses!

Many of those who failed to reach their goals claimed they had a "good excuse." All goal-seekers need to remember this Hindu proverb:

> How many doors to fame are shut
> By those bad fairies, "ifs" and "but?"

■ Be patient

Author Bo Bronson notes, "Most dreams take ten years to mature."

■ Walking uphill backwards

In his book, *Pronoia*, Rob Brezsny, tells of a day when he was out hiking and spotted a man walking backwards up a steep mountain. Rob told one of his friends about this strange observation. His friend told him it wasn't strange and, that she did it herself! She told him, "It's a psychological trick that helps make a steep ascent easier. You stay focused on how much you've already accomplished rather than being overwhelmed by the heights that are ahead of you." It sounds like good advice. When you are reaching for your goals, take time to reflect on the progress you've already achieved.

■ Keep moving

As you travel the road to your dream, keep moving. Every day try to do at least one thing that gets you closer to your goal. Cowboy philosopher, Will Rogers once said, "Even if you're on the right track, you'll get run over if you just sit there."

■ Goals = Happiness

Mountains of research find that the happiest people are those who are working towards positive goals. Author E. J. Bartek wrote, "Having a goal is a state of happiness."

Goals & Dreams QUIPS

■ It's up to you says Dr. Seuss

Never forget the powerful words of Dr. Seuss in his book, *Oh, The Places You'll Go*.

> *You have brains in your head,*
> *You have feet in your shoes,*
> *You can steer yourself*
> *In any directions you choose.*

■ Broken wings

The well-known poet, Langston Hughes reminds us, "Hold fast to your dreams, for if dreams die, life is a broken-winged bird that cannot fly."

■ As the crow flies

On your travel towards your goals and dreams, there will be setbacks. Seldom is the road to success flat and straight. There is a popular saying that goes, "As the crow flies." In his book, *Oliver Twist*, Charles Dickens wrote, "We cut over the fields....straight as the crow flies." The term, "as the crow flies" refers to a straight line between two points; it refers to the shortest distance between sites. Scientists have studied crows and noticed that they rarely fly straight. They are very curious birds that like to "zigzag" and observe things rather than fly straight. So, "as the crow flies," doesn't necessarily mean the shortest, most direct route. So, remember, seldom will your travels be short and direct.

■ We always seem to want what the other guy has

I am sure you've often heard the saying, "The grass isn't always greener on the other side of the fence." So many people focus their time and energy "wishing" they had what other people had instead of trying to improve themselves. You may wish you had what "the other guy" has but he might be wishing he had what you've got. Author Carl Burns wrote, "A child on a farm sees a plane fly overhead and dreams of a faraway place. A traveler on the plane sees the farmhouse and dreams of home." Concentrate on your goals and stop worrying about what others have that you don't.

■ Go Zoe!

In 1993, Zoe Koplowitz achieved her goal. She completed the New York City Marathon (26.2 miles). It took her 24 hours! She has multiple sclerosis and she did it on crutches.

Goals & Dreams

QUOTES

Goals & Dreams
QUOTES

"When one door of happiness closes, another opens; but often we look so long at the closed door that we do not see the one which has been opened for us."
-Helen Keller

☞**PRIMING THE PUMP:** Can you think of a time you failed to reach a goal? What happened? How did you react? Did you come up with excuses, get angry, and blame others or try again? Can failures make you a stronger person? How? Can you think of a "now famous" person who had several setbacks (closed doors) but eventually succeeded?

"If you follow every dream, you might get lost."
-Neil Young

☞**PRIMING THE PUMP:** Is it possible that someone may have too many dreams? Explain the advantages and disadvantages of having too few or too many dreams. What do you think Neil Young means by "getting lost?"

"No person has a right to rain on your dream."
-Marian Wright Edelman

☞**PRIMING THE PUMP:** Have you ever had someone tell you that your dream was foolish or that you couldn't do it? What was that dream and how did you react? When others "rained on your dream" did it motivate you to prove them wrong? Have you ever had such an "unbelievable" dream that you decided not to share it with others? Why haven't you shared it with others? Have you ever rained on someone's dream? If you did, how did that person react?

Goals & Dreams
QUOTES

"Gold medals aren't really made of gold. They're made of sweat, determination, and a hard-to-find alloy called guts."

-Dan Gable

☞**PRIMING THE PUMP:** What do you think Olympic gold medal wrestling champion Dan Gable means by "guts?" In order to make the Olympics, athletes must be determined. What do you think the word "determined" means? Is it possible to achieve goals without determination? Explain your answer.

"I do not try to dance better than anyone else. I only try to dance better than myself."

-Mikhail Baryshnikov

☞**PRIMING THE PUMP:** When trying to achieve our goals should we try to compare ourselves to others? For instance, if you wish to bet a great poet do you try to write like Maya Angelou or write like you? What are some disadvantages of always trying to compare ourselves with others? Should we try to be like others or strive for our own uniqueness? Why?

"My mother said to me, 'If you become a soldier, you'll be a general. If you become a monk, you'll end up as the pope.' Instead, I became a painter and wound up as me."

-Pablo Picasso

☞**PRIMING THE PUMP:** Picasso's mother had high expectations for him. How important is it to have great support from parents when reaching for your goals? What are some ways parents can support young people with their goals? Can young people still reach their goals without parental support? Explain your response. How do your parents react when you tell them your goals and dreams? Have you had a dream that you did not share with parents? Why not?

Q 137

Goals & Dreams QUOTES

"Goals are about the lightest things you have to travel with."
-Josh Ritter

☞**PRIMING THE PUMP:** What do you think singer, Josh Ritter means when he refers to goals as "light things?" If goals are light, then what are some heavy things people travel with? Can thoughts of defeat, loss, worry, and fear weigh heavy on a person? How?

"If you hit the target every time, the target is too near or too big."
-Tom Hirshfield

☞**PRIMING THE PUMP:** If Kirk only practices shooting baskets at an eight-foot basketball goal, will he be very effective playing in a game with a ten-foot goal? Explain your answer. What are some things that you are good at doing? Do you strive to improve at those things or are you content to perform at the same level all the time? How would our world be if our leaders settled for mediocre goals? If athletes didn't set high goals, would new records ever be set?

"Conditions are never just right. People who delay until all factors are favorable do nothing."
-William Feather

☞**PRIMING THE PUMP:** Is there ever a time when conditions are perfect for starting on a new plan? Have you ever heard people say things like, "It's too hot, I'll start tomorrow. It's too close to the holidays to start on a diet; I'll wait until January 1. I'll wait until I have enough money to buy a bike before I start an exercise program."? What 'perfect' conditions are you waiting for?

Goals & Dreams
QUOTES

"Don't say you don't have enough time. You have exactly the same number of hours per day that were given to Helen Keller, Pasteur, Michelangelo, Mother Teresa, Leonardo da Vinci, Thomas Jefferson and Albert Einstein."
-H. Jackson Brown

☞**PRIMING THE PUMP:** Do you think it is a valid excuse for someone to say, "I don't have enough time?" Explain your answer. Let's say you've decided on a goal that requires five hours a week. How could you adjust your schedule to "find" those five hours? There is a familiar saying that goes, "If something needs to be done, ask a busy person; they'll do it." How is it that the busier one is, they more likely he is to say yes when help is needed? How would things in the world be different if needy people were always told, "Sorry, I don't have enough time to help?"

"No matter where you're born or how much your parents have; no matter what you look like or what you believe in, you can still rise to become whatever you want; still go on to achieve great things; still pursue the happiness you hope for."
-Barack Obama

☞**PRIMING THE PUMP:** Barack Obama, U.S. Senator from Illinois made this statement at a college commencement ceremony in 2006. Do you agree or disagree with his comments and why? Do you think that people in our country have equal chances for success regardless of their race, color, religion, and income? If you don't think so, what changes need to be made to improve things?

"Champions aren't made in the gyms. Champions are made from something they have deep inside them—a desire, a dream, a vision. They have to have the skill and the will. But the will must be stronger than the skill."
-Muhammad Ali

☞**PRIMING THE PUMP:** Explain the difference between one's will and one's skill. Is it possible for, say a boxer, to have great skills but never become a champion? How? What are a couple of your great skills and how are you utilizing them?

139

Goals & Dreams
QUOTES

"Obstacles are those frightful things you see when you take your eyes off your goal."

-Henry Ford

☞**PRIMING THE PUMP:** Should all goal-setters expect a few obstacles and hurdles along the way? Can you think of a few successful people who overcame obstacles on their way to fame? If you focus too much time and attention on possible obstacles, will that help or hurt your chances for success? Explain your response. Often people like to use "what ifs" when starting goals. For instance they'll say things like, "What if it rains, What if I don't have time, What if no one helps me?" Explain how "what ifs" can become obstacles.

"You only grow as a human being if you're outside your comfort zone."

-Percy Cerutty

☞**PRIMING THE PUMP:** What do you think Percy Cerutty means by "your comfort zone?" If you never leave your comfort zone will you ever accomplish goals? Explain how leaving your comfort zone can be risky? Do you think that in reaching your goals you may have to take an occasional risk? Explain your response and give an example or two.

"You must have long-range goals to keep you from being frustrated by short-range failures."

-Charles C. Noble

☞**PRIMING THE PUMP:** As you strive to achieve your long-range goals do you foresee possible setbacks? If you anticipate these small failures, will you be better prepared to handle them? How? Let's say you have a goal to run a 5k (3.1 miles) race in six months, what are a few daily or weekly goals you would set?

Goals & Dreams
QUICK STARTERS

- *The Horse Named 'Never Say Die'*
- *She Donated $100 Million to Poetry Magazine*
- *Oh, No! I'm Three Miles Short of My Goal!*

NEVER SAY DIE

This is a story of a determined lady, a fast horse, and one of the most famous musical groups of all time. Musician Peter Best lived with his family in Liverpool, England in the late 1950's. His mother, Mona, had a dream of owning a coffee club where customers could enjoy beverages and hear local singers and bands perform. After a lengthy search she located a huge house for sale. The house had a large basement, just the perfect size for her coffee/music club. Her husband was not interested and refused to help her purchase the house. Mona was a very determined woman with a dream. She came up with a game plan. She gathered all her jewelry and other personal belongings and sold them at a pawn shop. She put the money in her purse and headed to the racetrack. For several hours she studied the list of horses that were scheduled to race that day. Near the bottom of the list was a horse named, Never Say Die. The horse was a 30-1 long shot but she liked its name because it reminded her of her goal to buy the house. She placed all her money on the race. Amazingly, Never Say Die won! She purchased the house.

In 1959 she opened her coffee club in the basement of her new house. Business was great. Many talented musicians played nightly. Even well-known Liverpool musicians John Lennon and George Harrison frequented the club. Mona's son Peter Best soon joined up with John, George, and eventually Paul McCartney to form the group called The Quarrymen. Peter was the band's drummer. Eventually Peter left the band and was replaced by another talented drummer, Ringo Star. The four musicians changed the name of their group to the Beatles…..and the rest is history!

If Mona had not pursued her dream, hocked her jewelry, bet on a long shot horse named Never Say Die, and opened her coffee club, then it is possible that the Beatles would have never created! We can all learn a lesson from Mona. Have a dream and never say die.

SHE DONATED $100 MILLION DOLLARS TO *POETRY* MAGAZINE

As a young girl, Ruth loved poetry. She read numerous poetry books and wrote hundreds of her own poems. She excelled in English class. Ruth felt that her gift was writing poems and she often dreamed of becoming a well-known poet.

One of her favorite publications to read was *Poetry* magazine. Eventually she started submitting poems to the magazine in hopes of becoming a published poet. Over the years the magazine had published poems by such titans as Dylan Thomas, William Butler Yates, and W. H. Auden. Ruth submitted many poems and they were all rejected. She received only handwritten rejection notes. She never lost confidence in her ability to write even though the *Poetry* magazine continually turned her down.

Ruth Lilly became heir to the Eli Lilly pharmaceutical fortune. She became one of the richest women in the world and she continued to write and submit poems without any luck. But she never got angry with the folks at the magazine. In fact, because of her love of poetry she donated $100 million to the magazine. She hoped her donation would help other young people to pursue the craft of writing poems. *Poetry* magazine now has an annual award called the Ruth Lilly Award that goes to promising young poets.

Even though her poems were constantly rejected, she didn't get upset or seek revenge towards the magazine. She never got published, but her kindness will help other young poets to get recognized.

Goals & Dreams
QUICK STARTERS

OH, NO! I'M THREE MILES SHORT OF MY GOAL!

What would you do if you realized, minutes before midnight on December 31, that you just missed one of your yearly goals? That's what happened to Adam Cohen. Let's find out what he did.

Adam tells his fascinating story in the January, 2006 issue of *Runner's World* magazine. Adam is a serious long distance runner who had a goal of running 2,000 miles in the year 2000. At 11:08 on December 31 he sat down to review his yearly running log and to celebrate his accomplishment; he ran 2,000 miles! But wait, he added up his miles again and realized he was three miles short; he only ran 1,997 miles. Oh, no! He needed to run three more miles. He looked out the window, it was cold and dark. He thought for a few minutes and then stood up and told his wife he was going out for a run.

It was 11:29 by the time he got on his shorts, sweatshirt, and running shoes. He ran the three miles, finishing at 11:53. As he walked up his driveway he could hear fireworks in the distance as neighbors celebrated the start of a new year. He celebrated his personal achievement.

Health & Nutrition

QUIPS

Q

Health & Nutrition
QUIPS

■ How many?

In July of 2006, Takeru 'The Tsunami' Kobayashi, from Japan, gulped down 53 hot dogs (with buns) in twelve minutes. That is the world's record.

■ Happy or unhappy?

Overheard at a fast food restaurant, "They call this a Happy Meal? With all the fat, sugar, and calories in it, they should call it an Unhappy Meal."

■ More fruit please

I've always been concerned about young people not eating enough fruit but I became even more concerned when I gave a second grader a banana. After looking it over he said to me, "Mr. Carr, how do you open it?"

■ The cheapest entertainment

Get outside more often; it's good for you and it's free. In Douglas Florian's book, *Insectlopedia*, he writes, "You don't need tickets to listen to crickets."

■ Sad but true

In the book, *Divorce Among the Gulls*, author William Jordan tells us, "The average American is said to spend 98% of the time indoors."

■ Be careful

From John Tayman's book, *The Colony*: "A healthy person suffers four thousand minor injuries in his lifetime—about one per week."

■ How is your sense of smell?

Yale University did a study of the most recognizable smells in the United States. The results: #1 coffee, #2 peanut butter, #3 Vicks Vapo-Rub, #4 crayons.

■ The last drop

Have you heard the slogan for Maxwell House Coffee? It goes, *'Good to the last drop.'* Credit goes to Theodore Roosevelt for the slogan. According to *Time* magazine Roosevelt was visiting Nashville, Tennessee in 1907. He was offered a cup of coffee at his hotel, and is said to have raved that the blend was "good to the last drop." The coffee company Maxwell House saw a slogan in the making and started using it in advertising in 1917.

■ Sugar

The Worldwatch Institute reports that the per-capita American sugar consumption today is 2.5 times what it was in 1961, with Americans consuming an average of 686 calories of sugar per day.

■ Portions are up

Food portion sizes have greatly increased in the last 25 years.

- salty snacks increased from 132 to 225 calories
- soft drinks increased from 114 to 193 calories
- french fries increased from 188 to 256 calories
- hamburgers increased from 389 to 486 calories

■ What are they eating?

The latest research reveals the top ten items being consumed by kids ages 6-19:

- carbonated beverages
- low-fat milk
- fruit drinks
- whole milk
- grain mixtures (pizza, pasta)
- meat mixtures (hamburgers, hot dogs)
- white potatoes (french fries)
- sugars, sweets (candy)
- cakes, cookies
- non-citrus juices

■ Eat at home

The American Stroke Association reports that children eat nearly twice as many calories (770) at restaurants as they do during a meal at home.

Health & Nutrition
QUIPS

■ Wow!

The American Stroke Association reports that American children spend about 45 hours per week using media (tv, computers, video games, etc) outside of school.

■ Where do we play?

In the April, 2000 issue of *Sun* magazine, Derrick Jensen revealed this disturbing fact, "Within a three-mile radius of South Central Los Angeles, there are 640 liquor stores and not one movie house or community center."

■ Enough sleep?

The National Sleep Foundation notes that only 20% of teens get the recommended 9 hours of sleep on school nights.

■ Night owls

Do you have trouble sleeping at night? Here's something to think about. Dr. Mel Levine, in his book, *A Mind at a Time*, writes, "Parents should not despair; some children with a sleep-arousal imbalance may turn out to be the next generation of night people. They may compose cello sonatas at 2:00 am, work the night shift at the BMW plant, or host an all-night radio rock show. Regrettably, during childhood, tomorrow's night owls are condemned to attend school with all the day kids. We don't yet offer night schools for night children."

Health & Nutrition
QUOTES

Health & Nutrition
QUOTES

"Physical fitness is not only one of the most important keys to a healthy body; it is the basis of dynamic and creative intellectual activity. The relationship between the soundness of the body and the activities of the mind is subtle and complex. Much is not yet understood, but we do know what the Greeks knew, that intelligence and skill can only function at the peak of capacity when the body is healthy and strong."

-John F. Kennedy

☞**PRIMING THE PUMP:** Movement and exercise send oxygen to the brain. The more oxygen, the better the brain works. What activities do you engage in that gets the blood and oxygen flowing? When you need a break from homework, what short-timed, quick activities do you try to "re-start" your brain? How does one's diet affect his or her ability to learn?

"If you are seeking creative ideas, go out walking. Angels whisper to a man when he goes for a walk."

-Raymond Inman

☞**PRIMING THE PUMP:** How can getting outside stimulate one's creativity? How do you enhance your creativity? What kinds of signals does your body send you, letting you know it is time for a break? Did you know that yawning is the body's way of getting more oxygen to the brain? When and where do you seem to do most of your yawning? What are some of the possible reasons you yawn in those settings?

Health & Nutrition
QUOTES

"Rest is not idleness, and to lie sometimes on the grass on a summer day listening to the murmur of the water, or watching the clouds float across the sky, is hardly a waste of time."

-John Lubbock

☞**PRIMING THE PUMP:** How do you "truly" rest? Where do you go to be alone and explain why you select that place? What are some of the benefits of seeking solitude? What emotional and physical symptoms can occur if you don't find time to rest and recharge your batteries?

"Before we can make deep changes in our lives, we have to look into our diet, our way of consuming. We have to live in such a way that we stop consuming the things that poison us and intoxicate us. Then, we will have the strength to allow the best in us to arise, and we will no longer be victims of anger, of frustration."

-Thich Nhat Hanh

☞**PRIMING THE PUMP:** How does one's diet affect his learning? How does diet affect one's emotions? Let's talk about breakfast. Nutritionists stress the importance of a good breakfast. What are the benefits of eating a good breakfast? What is your breakfast routine? What do you normally eat for breakfast on school days? Do you bring a mid-morning snack to school in your book bag, and if you do, what do you bring? What foods can hurt a student's learning and ability to focus?

Health & Nutrition
QUOTES

"It is a common experience that a problem difficult at night is resolved in the morning after the committee of sleep worked on it."

-John Steinbeck

☞**PRIMING THE PUMP:** What are some 'not-so-good' reasons for trying to solve big problems at night when you are tired? How is your frustration level affected when you are tired? Explain why it often seems that big problems at night turn in to little problems in the morning?

"Nearly all youngsters (97%) have at least one electronic item in their bedroom, such as television, computer, phone, or music device. Adolescents with four or more such items in their bedroom are much more likely than their peers to get an insufficient amount of sleep at night. They are also twice as likely to fall asleep in school and while doing homework."

-National Sleep Foundation

☞**PRIMING THE PUMP:** Count how many electronic devices you have in your bedroom, and then ask your parents how many they had in their bedrooms when they were children. What did you find out? Why do you think your parents had fewer devices than you? How do you think children entertained themselves years ago when they didn't have all of today's modern devices? If you were allowed only one electronic device in your room, which one would you select, and explain why? What are some possible reasons why children with more devices have more sleeping problems?

Health & Nutrition

QUICK STARTERS

- *What's in a Twinkie?*
- *The Magic Pill*

WHAT'S IN A TWINKIE?

Do you ever read the ingredients labels on junk food? If you do, have you ever noticed that some of the words are almost impossible to pronounce? Some of the ingredients are preservatives. They are added to extend the food item's shelf life. Food companies want their items to remain "fresh" as long as possible. Back in 1974, now retired teacher Roger Bennatti from Blue Hill, Maine conducted a lesson on preservation in his chemistry class. He, and his students, wanted to discover the shelf life of a Hostess Twinkie. Yes, the famous Twinkie—light, yellow cake with gooey cream filling—a fixture in the Junk Food Hall of Fame!

Bennatti placed the Twinkie on the top of the black board in his classroom. Every year his students studied the snack. It never spoiled; it always looked fresh and ready to eat. Bennatti taught for thirty years and retired in 2004, and the Twinkie never changed!   Roger Bennatti was an excellent teacher, but what his students remember the most about him and his lessons was the thirty year-old Twinkie!

So, the next time you reach for another helping of junk food, read the label. Ask yourself, "What did they put in it to make it last so long?"

Health & Nutrition
QUICK STARTERS

THE MAGIC PILL

How would you like to take a daily pill that would make you look better, feel better, have more energy, be more creative, help you get along better with others, and greatly improve your academic and athletic skills? Well, I've got some good news. There is a "magic" pill that can do all those things! Here is some more good news. The pill is free, non-addictive, has no negative side effects, it doesn't require a doctor's prescription, is totally natural, and you don't have to visit the drug store for refills. Here is even more good news! You already have one or two of these pills in your bedroom right now! What is this "magic" pill? It is the PILL-OW. Yes, the pillow, that soft, warm, comfortable cushion on your bed. If you keep your head on your pillow an extra hour every night, you'll reap the benefits mentioned above!

Let's look at some more reasons to utilize your magic pill:

- A recent study in the journal *Sleep* noted that in an experiment conducted by the National Institute of Health, children who were sleep-deprived had significantly more academic problems than those who had at least nine hours of sleep nightly. Those who got less than eight hours were more forgetful, had more trouble learning new lessons, and had the most problems paying attention.

- Dr. Carl Hunt, Director of the National Center on Sleep Disorders, notes, "Sleep does indeed matter. It helps school performance, learning, and memory. Children hear all the time that they need to eat healthy and be active. Getting a good night's sleep is just as important as diet and exercise."

- The National Institute of Health reminds us: Inadequate sleep can cause **decreases** in: performance, concentration, reaction times, consolidation of information and learning. Inadequate sleep causes **increases** in: memory lapses, accidents and injuries, behavior problems, and mood problems.

We all need more sleep. The sleep researcher, William Dement maintains that if Americans and Europeans of all ages would simply go to bed an hour earlier each night, and turn off the television no later than an hour before that, Western society would be happier and healthier.

155

Honesty & Sincerity
QUIPS

Honesty & Sincerity
QUIPS

■ Do you agree?

"He who steals a chicken while small, will grow up to steal on ox." (Chinese proverb)

■ An honest general

"Excuse me, sir; I cannot consent to receive pay for services I do not render." These words were spoken by General Robert E. Lee, explaining his rejection of a $10,000 a year salary to act as titular head of an insurance company after the Civil War.

■ Crazy Horse, a sincere warrior

"In another way, however, Crazy Horse was not the prototypical Lakota fighting man in that he didn't participate in a ritual called, wahtoglakapi, or 'to tell of one's victories.' It was a simple ritual in which fighting men were expected to recount their exploits on the battlefield. As a matter of fact, he barely talked about his exploits to his immediate family." *The Journey of Crazy Horse*, by Joseph M. Marshall.

■ Honest eyes

Can you tell if someone is not telling the truth by looking in his or her eyes? The following words were seen on a poster at a political campaign convention:

> **REAL EYES**
> **REALIZE**
> **REAL LIES**

■ How did the term 'to fudge' originate?

The verb to fudge means to lie. There are several theories on how that term originated. Here is the most common theory according to the book, *Verbivore's Feast*, by Chrysti the Wordsmith. In the 17th century England lived a sea merchant named Captain Fudge, nicknamed "Lying Fudge." Returning from his voyages, Lying Fudge brought with him many greatly exaggerated tales. He lied so much that other sailors, when they heard a great lie, would cry out, "You fudge it!"

■ Who let the cat out of the bag?

Have you ever asked a friend to keep a secret and she didn't? To let the cat out of the bag, means to reveal a secret. This saying originated many years ago in Europe according to Chrysti the Wordsmith. Young pigs were often sold as food by farmers at markets and fairs. The piglets, small enough to be carried home, were often placed in cloth bags. Looking to take advantage of gullible consumers, vendors substituted a cat for a pig. When the buyer got home to open the bag, he let the cat out of the bag.

■ Putting the cat back in the bag

The cowboy philosopher, Will Rogers noted, "Letting the cat out of the bag is a whole lot easier than putting it back." Oh, so true!

■ Our Pinocchio culture

Susan Tifft, professor of journalism at Duke University believes young people today are living in a time when they see so many successful grown-ups getting ahead by being dishonest. She calls this era the Pinocchio culture.

■ Ethics in 1890

Benjamin Comegys wrote a small book for young people called, *Primer of Ethics*, in 1890. He wrote, "Truth is sincerity; and in all we say and do, we must be sincere. We must not make false impressions, directly or indirectly." According to Comegys, these are five ways by which people mislead and deceive others by what they say:

- Saying a thing when we know it is not true.

- Saying a thing when we do not know whether it is true or not.

- Prevaricating. (Saying something which is not in itself strictly and absolutely false, but which is intended to convey a false meaning; as when a boy said that he had not a single marble in his pocket, while in fact he had many.)

- Misrepresenting. (We misrepresent when we tell a part of the truth and conceal the rest).

- Exaggeration.

Honesty & Sincerity
QUOTES

Q 159

Honesty & Sincerity
QUOTES

"Truth is completely spontaneous. Lies have to be taught."

-Buckminster Fuller

☞**PRIMING THE PUMP:** Do you believe in the theory that when you've done something wrong, you are better off telling the truth because you'll get into 'double-trouble' if later on it was discovered you lied? Can you share an experience where you were not honest at first and had to deal with stern consequences? Why do you think telling the truth is easier than telling a lie? How do young people learn to lie?

"What upsets me is not that you lied to me, but that from now on I can no longer believe you."

-Friedrich Nietzsche

☞**PRIMING THE PUMP:** What emotions do you usually feel when you find out one of your best friends lied to you? What upsets you more, when a friend lies to you or when an adult lies to you? Explain your response. How do you normally confront one of your friends who is dishonest with you? If someone lies to you, will you always find it difficult to believe him or her in the future?

"A lie can travel halfway around the world while the truth is putting on its shoes."

-Mark Twain

☞**PRIMING THE PUMP:** Can you think of a reason or two why lies travel faster than truths? When lies travel by you, how can you tell if they really are lies? When a lie travels to you, are you guilty sometimes of passing the lie on to others? What is your usual plan of action if untruths about you are traveling around?

Honesty & Sincerity
QUOTES

"The most exhausting thing in life is being insincere."

-Anne Morrow Lindbergh

☞**PRIMING THE PUMP:** Explain why being insincere can be so exhausting. Is it important to you that your friends be sincere? Why? How can you tell when someone is being insincere? For what reasons do you think some people are not always sincere?

"People will tolerate honest mistakes, but if you violate their trust you will find it very difficult to ever regain their confidence."

-Craig Weatherup

☞**PRIMING THE PUMP:** When your friends make honest mistakes, how important is it for you to forgive them? What are your thoughts on the saying, 'I forgive, but I will not forget?' If you make an honest mistake, why do you think it is important to apologize as soon as possible?

"If you ask people in India why it is that Mahatma Gandhi was able to do what he did in India, they will say they followed him because of his sincerity.....any time he made a mistake, even in his personal life, or even a decision that he made in the independence struggle, he came out in public and said, 'I made a mistake.'"

-Martin Luther King, Jr.

☞**PRIMING THE PUMP:** When people quickly and honestly admit their mistakes, do you tend to have more respect for them? Why? When you make mistakes, is it difficult or easy for you to admit it? Explain your response. What are your thoughts about people who never admit to making mistakes?

Honesty & Sincerity QUOTES

"If you get a reputation for being honest, you have 95 percent of the competition already beat."

-John Kenneth Galbraith

☞**PRIMING THE PUMP:** How long does it take for one to develop a reputation for being honest? How quickly can one's reputation change if he or she is caught being dishonest? Can you tell if a person is honest the first time you meet her? Explain. When you are deciding on which candidate to vote for, do you consider their reputation for honesty?

"The reason so few people are agreeable in conversation is that each is thinking more of what he is intending to say then what others are saying; and we never listen when we are planning to speak."

-Duc de la Rochefoucauld

☞**PRIMING THE PUMP:** Explain why it is important for you to have sincere listeners in your life? How do you feel when your parents, teachers, or friends are not 'truly' listening to you? When someone is talking to you, have you been guilty sometimes of not 'truly' listening? How do you think they felt knowing you weren't being sincere in the conversation?

Honesty & Sincerity
QUICK STARTERS

- *The Guy Who Brings the Bagels*
- *Sincere People Don't Hide Their Flaws*

THE GUY WHO BRINGS THE BAGELS

Paul Feldman is the guy who brings the bagels. His fascinating experiment with bagels and honesty has been featured in numerous newspapers, magazines, and the book, Freakonomics. Paul had a very good job working for the government in Washington, D.C., but he dreamed of having his own business. At his government job he would bring fresh bagels every morning for his employees. Soon neighboring office personnel would stop by Paul's office for bagels. His bagels became very popular and eventually he quit his job to sell them at office buildings throughout the capital area. At one time he was delivering 8,400 bagels a week to 140 companies and he was earning more money than he had ever made in his old job as a research analyst.

Paul's bagel sales were based on the honor system. He would leave the bagels at an office along with a basket. People could purchase a bagel and drop a dollar in the basket. Paul would stop by later in the day to collect unsold bagels and empty the money basket.

Throughout his years of selling his bagels he kept some interesting notes and statistics. Following are some of his fascinating facts that focus on people's honesty and the honor system.

■ The collection rate at the office where people knew him well was 95%. It seems that people who knew him were less likely to steal from him. In offices where he was unknown by most of the employees, the collections rates dropped as low as 80%.

■ In tall office buildings, usually the highest paid employees and executives have offices in the upper floors. Feldman found that the collection rate dropped as he went up the floors. In other words, the top level executives stole more than the lower paid workers on the lower floors.

■ Collection rates were the highest in the days immediately following the attack on the Twin Towers on 9/11.

■ Larger office buildings (those with more employees) tended to steal more than smaller offices with fewer employees (per capita).

■ Most "non-payers" were busiest during the holidays. More stealing took place around Christmas. Collection rates were poor around Thanksgiving as well.

■ There is some good news. Most people are honest. Paul's overall collection rate at all offices throughout the years was about 87%.

SINCERE PEOPLE
DON'T HIDE THEIR FLAWS

Many times we've heard the phrase, "Nobody's perfect." It's true! We've all made mistakes, under achieved at times, been unkind, and not helped others as much as we could. Some of us wish we were taller while some would like to be a couple inches shorter. Some people don't like the color of their hair, facial features or the sound of their voice. Many of us are great dancers and athletes, while others are extremely uncoordinated.

Many people accept themselves as they are and don't try to hide their flaws. I call these people, sincere. What you see is what you get! Others try to hide their flaws and I call these folks, insincere. Which kind of people do you like to associate with, the sincere or the insincere?

Have you ever wondered how the term 'sincere' came about? Well there is a theory, and it is based upon "hiding flaws." Author Mark Nepo, in his book, *The Exquisite Risk*, tells us of the origin. "If we trace the word (sincere) itself, we return to Roman times, where the Western form of the word originated. It comes from the Latin sin cere, meaning "without wax." During the Italian Renaissance, sculptors were as plentiful as plumbers, and markets selling marble and other stones were as prevalent as hardware stores. Frequently, stone sellers would fill the cracks in flawed stones with wax and try to sell them as flawless. Thus, an honest stone seller became known as someone who was sincere— one who showed his stone without wax, cracks and all." Mark Nepo adds, "A sincere person, then, came to mean someone who is honest and open enough to hide their flaws."

Kindness & Compassion
QUIPS

Kindness & Compassion
QUIPS

■ I'm sorry

According to an opinion poll commissioned by the Parker Brothers game company, Americans say, "I'm sorry" an average of only 5 times a month."

■ Kindness

Writer Henry James said, "Three things in human life are important. The first is to be kind. The second is to be kind. And the third is to be kind."

■ Polite to the very end

"Sir, forgive me, I did not do it deliberately," were the last words spoken by Queen Marie Antoinette. She said those words to the executioner near the guillotine after she accidentally stepped on his foot.

■ Heart trouble

The late, great comedian, Bob Hope said, "If you haven't any charity in your heart, you have the worst kind of heart trouble."

■ George Washington Carver's epitaph

He could have added fortune to fame,
but caring for neither,
he found happiness and honor
in being helpful to the world.

■ One a day

Charley Willey says, "Make one person happy each day and in forty years you will have made 14,600 human beings happy for a little time, at least."

■ Even with kindness, be careful

In his book, *The Exquisite Risk*, Mark Nepo tells the story of a man who came across a butterfly half-born from its cocoon. It seemed to be struggling and so, trying to help, he gently exhaled his warm breath on it. Sure enough, his breath hastened its birth, but the butterfly fell to the ground, unable to fly. Its premature birth left its wings deformed.

Kindness & Compassion
QUIPS

■ Say 'thank you'

Author William A. Ward reminds us, "God gave you a gift of 86,400 seconds today. Have you used one to say "Thank you?"

■ Be kind to the hungry, close the window

In modern Turkey people are encouraged to keep their windows closed when cooking because the smell might make the poor, hungry people in the streets difficult to bear. Also, Turks who barbecue outside often take a plate of food to their neighbors.

■ Don't despair, truth and love always wins

Mohandas Gandhi offers these encouraging words, "When I despair, I remember that all through history, the way of truth and love always won. There have been murderers and tyrants, and for a time they can seem invincible. But in the end they always fail. Think of it, always."

■ It was only a smile

> *It was only a smile,*
> *And little it cost in the giving.*
> *But like morning light, it scattered the night,*
> *And made the day worth living.*
>
> -anonymous

■ Maige's tricycle

Father Joseph Healey visited the country of Tanzania many years ago. He met a young boy named Maige who had crippled legs. He propelled himself by using his hands and sliding along on his knees. Despite his handicap he never missed Mass on Sundays. The kind Father decided to buy him a tricycle. It was quite unusual, with regular-sized bike tires. The pedals were up front and are propelled by one's hands. When the tricycle arrived, Maige climbed on a pedaled away. The whole village cheered for him.

Kindness & Compassion
QUIPS

■ Trail Angels

There is 'Trail Magic' all along the 2,173 miles of the Appalachian Trail. Trail Magic is one of the most motivational acts that keeps hikers going. Trail Magic involves special people, known as Trail Angels, who leave gifts of food along the trail. Imagine you are a tired, hungry hiker and you come across a treat of soda, candy bars, or even fresh biscuits. Trail Angels also sit and wait for the hikers to see if they need a ride to town or a hot shower. One such angel is a man named Ed Williams who, every morning from mid-May to mid-July, drives 22 miles to bring fresh-baked biscuits, home-made apple butter, veggies and apples to hikers.

■ A desire to help others

When Deborah Ellis traveled throughout Africa to interview children for her book, *Our Stories, Our Songs: African Children Talk about AIDS*, she was amazed to discover that almost all the children, whose parents died from AIDS, wanted to be doctors or nurses when they grew up. They had a great desire to help others who were effected by AIDS.

Kindness & Compassion
QUOTES

Kindness & Compassion
QUOTES

"I've learned that people will forget what you said. People will forget what you did, but people will never forget how you made them feel."

-Maya Angelou

☞**PRIMING THE PUMP:** What are some things people say or do that make you feel bad? Who are some people in your life that always seem to say or do things that help you to feel good about yourself? When others make you feel bad, do you tell them? Can you think of a time you may have said something that made another person feel bad. What did you do? Did you apologize?

"Seek to do good, and you will find that happiness will run after you."

-James Freeman Clarke

☞**PRIMING THE PUMP:** What are some things that you do for others that make you happy? Do you think selfish, greedy, self-centered people can ever be truly happy? Explain your response. Have you ever volunteered at a hospital, shelter for the homeless, food bank, or other community agency? What did you do and how did you feel when you finished?

"How wonderful it is that nobody needs to wait a single moment before starting to improve the world."

-Anne Frank

☞**PRIMING THE PUMP:** What are some things that you can do to improve the world that doesn't cost you a penny? Think of something you'd like to do to improve the world when you get older and have money to do it? What are some things you can say or do for you family today that can have even a tiny impact on improving the world? If you could travel anywhere in the world to help people, where would you go and why?

Q 171

Kindness & Compassion
QUOTES

"Never ruin an apology with an excuse."

-Kimberly Johnson

☞**PRIMING THE PUMP:** Can you give an example of what it means to ruin an apology with an excuse? When one of your friends hurts your feelings would you rather he or she simply say, "I'm sorry" or give you an excuse for their behavior? Explain your response. Is it easy or difficult for you not to follow an "I'm sorry" with an excuse?

"Every man must decide whether he will walk in the creative light of altruism or the darkness of destructive selfishness. This is the judgment. Life's persistent and most urgent question is, 'What are you doing for others?'"

-Martin Luther King, Jr.

☞**PRIMING THE PUMP:** What is altruism? How do you answer the question, "What are you doing for others? Explain how selfishness can be destructive?

"Nothing is ever lost by courtesy. It is the cheapest of the pleasures, costs nothing and conveys much. It pleases him who gives and him who receives, and thus, like mercy, it is twice blessed."

-Erastus Wiman

☞**PRIMING THE PUMP:** What are a few simple courtesies that we could all do that would please others? Can you think of a recent incident in which you encountered a rude person? How do you react to his or her rudeness? What do you think Wiman means when he calls courtesy a "pleasure?" Have you ever smiled and said 'hello' to someone and they did not acknowledge you? How did you feel? Do you believe you should be courteous to everyone, even those people you do not like? When someone is rude to you and you return the rudeness, will that help or hurt the chances of the two of you getting along better with each other? Explain your response.

Kindness & Compassion
QUOTES

"Sometimes I think that all we are learning in life is that we are happy when we are kind and unhappy when we are not. We resist the lesson because it's so simple it's insulting."

-Hugh Prather

☞**PRIMING THE PUMP:** How can kindness improve one's happiness? Does Prather's simple formula work for you; in other words, do find yourself a happier person when you are kind? When you are feeling down, what are a few kind things you can do that might help you to feel better?

"What do we live for if not to make life less difficult for each other?"
-George Eliot

☞**PRIMING THE PUMP:** Go ahead, answer Eliot's question. What are some things you do to make life less difficult for others? Who are some adults in your life that help you? Can you list several professionals at your school whose job it is to help make things less difficult for students?

"If it is your partner who is angry, just listen. Listen and do not react. Do your best to practice compassionate listening. Do not listen for the purpose of judging, criticizing, or analyzing. Listen only to help the other person express himself and find some relief from his suffering."

-Thich Nhat Hanh

☞**PRIMING THE PUMP:** When you are very upset and want to "vent" do you want your 'listener' to just listen or give advice? How do you feel when you are venting and your 'listener' starts telling you what you should do or should have done? Are you able to listen to an upset person without interrupting and giving too much advice? What would be some characteristics of a compassionate listener?

Q 173

Kindness & Compassion
QUOTES

"My dad always taught me these words: care and share. That's why we put on clinics. The only thing I can do is try to give back. If it works, it works."

-Tiger Woods

☞**PRIMING THE PUMP:** Many famous athletes, like Tiger Woods, 'give back.' What does it mean to 'give back'? Can you think of other athletes who have given some of their time and/or money to help others? Who are they and what did they do? Do you think it is important for famous, rich individuals to share their wealth? Why? If you were wealthy, what group, or groups of people would you help?

"I shall pass through this world but once. Any good therefore that I can show to another human being, let me do it now."

-Mahatma Gandhi

☞**PRIMING THE PUMP:** What are some things that you do daily to show kindness and compassion? Have you ever regretted not saying or doing something nice for someone? What happened? When others show kindness to you, how do you let them know it was appreciated?

"Only eyes washed by tears can see clearly."

-Louis Mann

☞**PRIMING THE PUMP:** What do you think Louis Mann means by his quote? Do you think it is a sign of weakness when people cry? Explain your response. Can you think of a time recently when you witnessed an act of kindness that made you cry? Can you think of a time recently in which you witnessed an act of rudeness or cruelty that made you cry?

Kindness & Compassion
QUICK STARTERS

- **From Rudeness to Compassion**
- **Put on your Flashers!**
- **An Incredible Act of Forgiveness**
- **I'm Sorry; I thought you were a Pickpocket**

Q 175

FROM RUDENESS TO COMPASSION

A few years ago, Sue Hubbell wrote an article for *Time* Magazine about truckers. She traveled the country studying and interviewing the drivers and visiting truck stops. She witnessed many interesting things, but there was one experience that she will never forget.

Sue visited one truck stop where four burley drivers sat together at the counter. It was very busy and a recently hired young waitress was doing her best to wait on the demanding men. The drivers decided to have some fun at her expense. They started to hassle her. One yelled to her, "Hey, I've got salt in my sugar!" She sampled it and agreed that the sugar tasted salty. As she apologized and headed back to the kitchen the truckers laughed at their little joke. When she returned, another trucker complained that there was salt in his sugar. Again she apologized and the men chuckled. Then a third driver had a similar complaint. The young waitress was doing the best she could but the more upset and nervous she got; the more the men were amused.

Soon the four truckers started complaining about how long it was taking for their meals to arrive. She again did her best to appease the men, but they didn't let up. She got so upset that she spilled a glass of water and then sat down and cried. Sue Hubbell overheard her saying, "My husband left me with the kids. This is the only job I could get. The state has told me if I don't keep bringing in the money, they're going to put my kids in a foster home." The truckers heard her sad tale and snuck out the side door without eating their $3.95 breakfasts.

As Sue was comforting the distraught waitress she looked at the abandoned counter and noticed that each trucker left the waitress a $20 bill. Sue said, "Honey, look what the truckers left you!"

Kindness & Compassion
QUICK STARTERS

PUT ON YOUR FLASHERS!

Daniel Gottlieb is a practicing psychologist, family therapist, writer, and columnist in Philadelphia. He continues to be very successful in his career even though he is confined to a wheelchair. About twenty-five years ago he was paralyzed from the waist down as the result of a terrible car accident. Thanks to a specially-designed van he is still able to drive. In his book, *Letters to Sam*, he tells about the day he struggled to drive home from a lecture. His story goes from frustration to compassion.

As he steered his van onto the busy four-lane expressway at rush hour, he began having spasms and was losing body control. He slowed down and kept to the right, but aggressive, angry drivers kept blasting their horns at him. Some gave him the middle finger and shouted out obscenities. Daniel was determined to get home because he was in pain. If only the other drivers on the road knew of his dilemma, they wouldn't be so rude he thought.

Then a strange thing happened. He decided to put on his four-way flashers. Once he put on his flashers, even though he was only going thirty miles an hour, no one honked, yelled, and no more fingers. He wrote, "When I put on my flashers, I was saying to the other drivers, 'I have a problem here. I am vulnerable and doing the best I can.' And everyone understood. Several times, in my rearview mirror, I saw drivers who wanted to pass. They couldn't get around me because of the stream of passing traffic. But instead of honking or tailgating, they waited, knowing the driver in front of them was in some way weak."

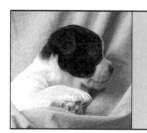
AN INCREDIBLE ACT OF FORGIVENESS

In 1996 a young gang member was transporting drugs and weapons when he was pulled over by a state patrol officer. The sixteen year-old took out a gun and shot the officer. Luckily he didn't die, and the gang member was sent to prison for 68 years for attempted first-degree murder. When the young inmate was in prison, other gang members looked up to him because he shot a police officer. He enjoyed the special attention

Three years later his mother died. He was shocked and secluded himself from others. Then to his amazement, the officer that he shot wrote him a letter expressing his condolences. The officer said he had completely recovered from the shot and that he forgave him. The officer also said he would go to court to see if the judge would shorten his prison sentence. According to the story published in the April, 2004 issue of *Spirituality & Health*, the prisoner noted, "I was shocked. Such compassion and forgiveness had never been shown to me before. As I read the letter I wept for the first time since I was a child."

The police officer kept his word. He went to court and helped convince the judge to decrease the years from 68 to 15! Now the young man looks forward to his release and he stated, "I have quit the gang, with great difficulty, and begun my search for a compassion equal to that officer's."

Kindness & Compassion
QUICK STARTERS

I'M SORRY; I THOUGHT YOU WERE A PICKPOCKET

Lucy Morgan Beard was a school teacher in North Carolina in the late 1800's. She loved to travel throughout the United States and Europe. Her students loved to hear stories from her travels. Lucy had special traits of positive opinions, honesty, fair play, and her willingness to change her mode of thinking when convinced she was in the wrong. One incident that occurred in London helps to illustrate her positive character traits.

When in London she wanted to visit one of the more dangerous parts of town. She was warned about pickpockets, young thugs, polluted streets, and other unsafe elements. She was especially warned about being very cautious with money and valuables. She stuck her pocketbook in her stocking. As she was walking up the street a dirty, poor man dressed in rags came up to her and said, "Lady, you dropped this." Being wary, she told him to. "Keep your distance!" When she turned around she recognized her pocketbook in his hand. She apologized and took her pocketbook. She was so thankful and had to think of a way to reward him. She ended up sending him some money every month as long as she lived. She even left him some money when she died. Her gratitude helped the young man escape poverty.

Motivation

QUIPS

Motivation QUIPS

■ Ifs & buts

"How many doors to fame are shut by those bad fairies, *ifs & buts*?"

-Hindu proverb

■ You better be running!

This popular African tale reminds of the importance of being self-motivated. Every morning in Africa, when a gazelle wakes up it knows it must run faster than the fastest lion or it will be killed. Every morning in Africa, when a lion wakes up it knows it must outrun the slowest gazelle or it will starve to death. It doesn't matter whether you're a lion or a gazelle. When the sun comes up, you'd better be running.

■ Concentrate

When the great tennis player Martina Navratilova was asked how she got to be so good, she replied, "I concentrate on my concentrating."

■ Six hours a day

One day an aggressive sports reporter was questioning the famous cyclist, Lance Armstrong, about his suspected use of performance-enhancing drugs. The reporter asked, "Lance, what are you on?" An angry Armstrong replied, "I'll tell you what I'm on….I'm on my bike 6 hours a day. That's why I'm successful."

■ Motivating mentors

Occasionally a parent or teacher will appoint someone to be a young person's mentor. The mentor helps with schoolwork and he or she acts as a motivator as well. How did the term 'mentor' originate? Well, it seems that the fabled Greek hero Odysseus had to leave his family to fight in a war. He was very concerned about his son's welfare while he was gone so he provided him with a guardian. The guardian was a trusted friend of the family named Mentor.

Motivation QUIPS

■ You got to fish in order to eat

Here is a cute Chinese rhyme that stresses the importance of being motivated to do some work:

> *This one makes a net,*
> *This one stands and wishes.*
> *Would you like to make a bet*
> *Which one gets the fishes?*

■ Keep swinging!

The Hall of Fame home run hitter Mickey Mantle tells why it is important to keep swinging….you might hit a few homers! He once said, "During my 18 years I came to bat almost 109,000 times. I struck out about 1,700 times and walked about 1,800 times. You figure a ball player will average 500 at-bats a season. That means that I played 7 years in the major leagues without even hitting the ball."

■ Act on your great ideas

If you think you have a great idea, go for it. Curtis Grant puts a humorous twist of this thought. He says, "Having the world's best idea will do you no good unless you act on it. People who want milk shouldn't sit on a stool in the middle of a field in hopes that a cow will back up to them."

■ Marathon motivation

Author Heather Lende, in her book, *If You Lived Here, I'd Know Your Name*, tells of a doctor's visit that motivated her to run a marathon. "I was visiting in a doctor's office in Juneau, looking at the framed documents on the wall while he lectured me about getting more exercise. I skipped over the medical diplomas and settled on a Portland marathon finisher's certificate. It said, 3 hours, forty-five minutes. I memorized it and vowed to start training for a marathon….I ran the Portland Marathon a year later and beat my doctor's time by twenty minutes!"

■ Risks

"Take risks. If you win you'll be happy; if you lose, you will be wise." –anonymous

Motivation

QUOTES

Motivation
QUOTES

"You can't propel yourself forward by patting yourself on the back."

-Steve Prefontaine

☞**PRIMING THE PUMP:** Once you achieve a goal, do you sit back and gloat or do you immediately start on another goal? What are your thoughts about people who brag about their accomplishments? Explain why you think it is important for people to 'always' have at least one goal to shoot for?

"Many people say I'm the best women's soccer player in the world. I don't think so. And because of that, someday I just might me."

-Mia Hamm

☞**PRIMING THE PUMP:** When you do well, whom do you wish to please the most: parents, teachers, friends, yourself? Explain your response. What are some possible negative consequences of always judging your efforts solely on what others think? If others think you are "the best" at something, is that enough to make you content, or do your continue to set higher standards for yourself?

"Who hits more practice balls every day than any other golfer? Guess what? It's Tiger Woods."

-Chris Carmichael

☞**PRIMING THE PUMP:** Is it surprising to you that Tiger Woods practices more than any other golfer? Explain your answer. What can happen to people, such as Tiger, who become content with their present accomplishments? What is a special gift or talent that you have and how are you nurturing it?

Motivation
QUOTES

"If you want something you've never had, you must do something you've never done."

-Tom Carr

☞**PRIMING THE PUMP:** What are your thoughts about people who are always talking about what they want to accomplish, but never do anything about it? What major accomplishment do you dream of achieving, and presently, what are you doing about it? Let's say you want to be a good poet, singer, artist, or athlete, what are some things you would have to give up while you are working on your dreams and goals?

"Don't feel entitled to anything you didn't sweat and struggle for."

-Marian Wright Edelman

☞**PRIMING THE PUMP:** What does it mean to be 'entitled to'? If you worked hard several days to earn money to buy a bike, do you think you'd take better care of it, as opposed to a bike that was given to you by your parents? Explain your response. What gives you a better feeling, getting a A in a class in which you did little work, or getting a B in a class in which you had to work real hard? What was your most recent accomplishment that involved "sweating" and how did you do it?

"The person who is waiting for something to turn up might start with their shirt sleeves."

-Garth Henrichs

☞**PRIMING THE PUMP:** Share with others a recent accomplishment in which you had to "roll up your sleeves." Are you the type of person who, a) complains about litter, or b) picks it up? Explain your answer. What are a few activities in which you "rolled up your sleeves" to help at home or in your community? Share your feelings about helping others.

Q 185

Motivation
QUOTES

"When I'd get tired and want to rest, I'd wonder what my next opponent was doing. I'd wonder if he was still working out. I tried to visualize him. When I could see him still working, I'd start pushing myself. When I could see him in the shower, I'd push myself harder."

-Dan Gable

☞**PRIMING THE PUMP:** Dan Gable was an Olympic gold medalist in wrestling who was known for working harder and practicing more than his opponents. When you find yourself preparing for a competitive event, do you often think about how much your opponents are practicing? If you do think about how much they are practicing, how can that help? Practicing is important, but can you think of some negative aspects of practicing too much? Recently, what is something you have been practicing a lot and how do you fit it into your schedule?

"Everyone who's ever taken a shower has had an idea. It's the person who gets out of the shower, dries off, and does something about it who makes a difference."

-Nolan Bushnell

☞**PRIMING THE PUMP:** Some people do come up with great ideas in the shower. Where are you when your creative juices start flowing? What is a neat idea you've had lately, and how did you act on it? Some people write their ideas down on a piece of paper. Can you think of a few reasons why they do that?

"Undertake something that is difficult; it will do you good. Unless you try to do something beyond what you already mastered, you will never grow."

-Robert E. Osborn

☞**PRIMING THE PUMP:** Recently, what was something you accomplished that was very difficult and how did you feel about? Does ten year-old Billy have a better chance improving his basketball skills if he continues to play with other ten year-olds or with boys a bit older than he is? Explain your answer. Think of a few reasons some people hesitate to attack difficult things. While you are learning new things, how can mistakes and setbacks help you grow?

Motivation
QUOTES

"The great composer does not set to work because he is inspired, but becomes inspired because he is working. Beethoven, Bach, and Mozart settled down day after day to the job in hand with as much regularity as an accountant settles down each day to figures. They didn't waste time waiting for inspiration."
-Ernest Newman

☞**PRIMING THE PUMP:** Which theory do you think leads to more accomplishments and why: Work leads to inspiration or inspiration leads to work? How different would the world be if everyone waited for inspiration to get them motivated to work? You might not be inspired to be a long distance runner, but is it possible that if you went out running every day for a month, that you might enjoy it and become inspired to become a long distance runner?

"It's my job. I love it. I wouldn't ride it if I didn't. But it's incredibly hard work, full of sacrifices. And you have to be able to go out there every single day."
-Lance Armstrong

☞**PRIMING THE PUMP:** Lance mentions sacrifices. What do you think were some sacrifices he had to make in order to win his seven Tours de France? One of the reasons Lance Armstrong was so successful was because he was passionate about cycling. Was does it mean to be passionate? What is something for which you have great passion?

"I want to be remembered as the guy who gave his all whenever he was on the football field. I want people to know that Walter Payton will be putting out on every play."
-Walter Payton

☞**PRIMING THE PUMP:** If you don't reach a goal, is it easier to accept it knowing that you gave it your all rather that going at it half-hearted? Please explain. Would you prefer to be remembered for your successes and failures or, for your persistence and work ethic? Quite often we'll hear an athlete on television say, "I gave 110%." How can that be possible?

187

Motivation
QUOTES

"It's so important to believe in yourself. Believe that you can do it, under any circumstances. Because if you believe you can, then you really will. That belief just keeps you searching for the answers, and then pretty soon you get it."

-Wally "Famous" Amos

☞**PRIMING THE PUMP:** How important is self-confidence as you attempt to reach a goal? When you don't achieve your goal or complete a required task, do others want to hear your excuses? Why not? What is your opinion of those who rarely, if ever, use excuses? What are some common excuses you hear from those who don't achieve their goals?

"The great men of the centuries past were never in a hurry and that is why the world will never forget them in a hurry."

-Cecil Webb-Johnson

☞**PRIMING THE PUMP:** Explain the importance of being patient while attempting to reach a goal. Can you think of at least one famous person in history that was successful because he or she took years to achieve his or her goal? What did that person achieve and how was patience an asset. When you set goals are you realistic with time frames? What are some negative consequences that can occur if you don't give yourself enough time?

Motivation

QUICK STARTERS

- *12 Hours a Day for 7 Months*
- *The Guy in the Glass*

Q 189

12 HOURS A DAY FOR 7 MONTHS

In 2002, Rick Warren finished writing the book, *The Purpose-Drive Life*. Within three years the book sold over twenty-three million copies. It pre-sold five hundred thousand copies. It averaged more than a million copies in sales a month in its first two years. According to the November 12, 2005 New Yorker, "Of those who bought the book as individuals, nearly half bought more than one copy, sixteen per cent have bought four to six copies, and seven per cent have bought ten or more." *The Purpose-Driven Life* is now among the best-selling nonfiction hardcover books in American history.

Warren knew his book was a good idea but never expected it to be so successful. He tells people, "I'm just not that good a writer; I'm a pastor." The *New Yorker* article tells how he had to motivate himself to finish the book. He locked himself in his office, twelve hours every day for seven months! He reported, "I would get up at four-thirty, arrive at my special office at five, and I would write from five to five. I'm a people person, and it about killed me to be alone. By 11:30 my Attention Deficit Disorder would kick in and I would do anything not to be there."

Rick had to make some sacrifices and practically force himself to write, but his motivation and self-discipline paid off. One other interesting note about him and his book is that he and his wife decided to reverse tithe, giving away ninety percent of the tens of millions they earned.

Motivation
QUICK STARTERS

THAT GUY IN THE GLASS

At times, people are motivated to help themselves, while at others times they are motivated to help others. For example, an Olympic swimmer may spend years training in the pool in order to improve his time by a half-second in hopes of winning a medal. Then there are people like Vinoba Bhave who focus practically all their time and energy on helping others. Vinoba was a monk who had previously worked with Gandhi. He worked mainly for land reform in India and made a valiant attempt to get land for the poorest of the poor, the Untouchables. He walked all over India, talking to landowners, saying that land – like air, sun, and water – is a free gift from God, and that every person has a right to the earth. His goal was to acquire 50 million acres for the Untouchables. He started his movement in 1955, and for 30 years, until his death in 1985, he walked back and forth across India. He did not get his 50 million acres, but he did get 4 million acres for the poor; he did his best!

Whether you are an athlete, writer, dancer, scientist, or an activist like Vinoba Bhave, can you look at yourself in the mirror and say, "I did my best?" Yes, it is nice to do things to please others, but occasionally ask yourself, "Am I pleased with me and my effort?" Following is a poem by an anonymous writer that I found in the book, *Season of Life*, by Jeffrey Marx. It might be a good idea for all of us to read it once in a while.

The Guy in the Glass

When you get what you want in your struggle for self
and the world makes you king for a day,
then go to the mirror and look at yourself
and see what that guy has to say.

For it isn't your mother, brother or friends
whose judgment you must pass.
The person whose verdict counts most in your life
is the one staring back in the glass.

You can go down the pathway of years
receiving pats on the back as you pass,
but your final reward will be heartaches and tears,
if you cheated that guy in the glass.

Perseverance

QUIPS

Perseverance QUIPS

■ Snails

Theologian Charles Haddon Spurgeon reminds us, "By perseverance the snails reached the Ark."

■ Consider the postage stamp

"Consider the postage stamp, my son. It secures success through its ability to stick to one thing 'till it gets there." -Josh Billings

■ Persevere, you can do it!

Try this tongue twister. According to the Guiness Book of World Records, it is the hardest one.
The sixth sick sheik's sixth sheep's sick.

■ Maybe this one is easier

The skunk sat on the stump.
The stump thunk the skunk stunk,
And the skunk thunk the stump stunk.

■ Maxey Flier never gave up

Maxey graduated from law school at the age of 36 and took the bar exam for the first time. He didn't pass, but he kept trying. He took it again, and again, and again but couldn't pass. Finally, on the forty-eighth try, he passed. At the age of 68 he officially became a lawyer.

■ Say that again

Here is a bulletin that was published by the Prague government a few years ago. Does it make sense to you? Read it again!

Because Christmas Eve falls on a Thursday, the day has been designated a Saturday for work purposes. Factories will close all day, with stores open a half day only. Friday, December 25, has been designated a Sunday, with factories and stories open all day. Monday, December 28, will be a Wednesday for work purposes. Wednesday, December 30, will be a business Friday. Saturday, January 2, will be a Sunday, and Sunday, January 3 will be a Monday.

Q 193

Perseverance QUIPS

■ Go ahead and sweat

Dan Gable, gold-medal Olympian wrestler says, "No one ever drowned in sweat."

■ Perseverance can solve the 'puzzler'

There's a famous fast-food restaurant you can go to where you can order chicken nuggets. They come in boxes of various sizes. You can only buy them in a box of 6, a box of 9, or a box of 20. So, if you are really hungry you can buy 20, if you are moderately hungry you can buy 9, and if there are more of you, maybe you buy 20 and divide them up. Using these order sizes, you can order, for example, 32 pieces of chicken if you wanted. You'd order a box of 20 and two boxes of 6. Here's the question. What is the largest number of nuggets that you cannot order? For example, if you wanted, say 37 of them, could you get 37? No. Is there a larger number of chicken nuggets that you cannot get? And if there is, what number is it? (The answer is at the bottom of the page).

■ I think I can, I think I can

Researchers have found that the Little Blue Engine was onto something when he said, "I think I can, I think I can, I think I can." A study found that positive self-talk (telling yourself you can) was the most effective of several motivational techniques.

■ Keep going and going

Actor Sylvester Stallone said, "I am not the smartest or most talented person in the world, but I succeeded because I keep going, and going, and going."

*answer to the puzzler: 43

■ The clever poet

The poet named, Sparrow, submitted many poems to *The Sun*, and kept getting rejected. He got clever and sent in this poem. It got published!

> *Over and over,*
> *I have submitted poems*
> *to this magazine.*
>
> *Over and over,*
> *the editor*
> *has rejected them.*
>
> *Finally,*
> *he accepted*
> *this poem.*

Perseverance

QUOTES

Perseverance QUOTES

"I attribute my success to this; I never gave or took an excuse."

-Florence Nightingale

☞**PRIMING THE PUMP:** What do you think is the definition of the word 'excuse'? How do you usually feel when people didn't keep their word, or do what they promised you, then they gave you an excuse? What will eventually happen to children if their parents and teachers keep letting them get by with excuses? Can you think of an example of a 'valid' excuse?

"Let me tell you the secret that has led me to my goal. My strength lies solely in my tenacity."

-Louis Pasteur

☞**PRIMING THE PUMP:** What is "tenacity?" What are some animals that we consider to be tenacious? What are some characteristics of people who are tenacious? Have you ever been tenacious at something? What was it and how successful were you? How difficult is it be get tenacious about something for which you are not passionate?

"Good things will come to me, but I will have to work hard and work all the time to make it happen."

-Sue Bender

☞**PRIMING THE PUMP:** How important is it to be optimistic as you work on your goals? What are some reasons why pessimistic people seldom achieve their goals? What is a "good thing" that you anticipate will happen to you if you work hard?

Perseverance QUOTES

"Press on. Nothing in the world can take the place of perseverance. Talent will not; nothing is more common than unsuccessful men with talent. Genius will not; unrewarded genius is almost a proverb. Education will not; the world is full of educated derelicts. Persistence and determination alone are omnipotent."

-Calvin Coolidge

☞**PRIMING THE PUMP:** President Calvin Coolidge has some strong comments on how perseverance is more important than talent, genius, and education. Do you agree with him? Explain your response. In sports we often hear the term "upset." What is an "upset?" Can you think of a recent upset in the world of sports? Lauren is the best speller in the eighth grade class, but she lost to Shameka in the Spelling Bee. How could that have happened?

"Don't quit my father advised me as I agonized over whether to drop a college class. 'Why not?" I asked. 'Because once you find out how easy it is to quit, you'll keep doing.' He was right."

-Leslie Toombs

☞**PRIMING THE PUMP:** Does quitting become easier the more often you do it? What does the future hold for a young person who falls into the habit if being a quitter? How do you usually react to a friend who always quits when he or she starts to lose a game? Many adults quit their jobs before they find another one. Would you do that? Explain your answer.

"I've always believed that if you put in the work, the results will come. I don't do things half-heartedly because I know if I do, then I can expect half-hearted results."

-Michael Jordan

☞**PRIMING THE PUMP:** What does the term 'half-hearted' mean? What are some activities in which you put your heart into? What are some chores, school subjects, or other activities that you do not enjoy so you don't put your heart into them? Do you think it is possible to put your whole heart into everything you do? Explain your response.

Perseverance
QUOTES

"No one gets an ironclad guarantee of success. Certainly, factors like opportunity, luck, and timing are important. But the backbone of success is usually found in old-fashioned, basic concepts like hard work, determination, good planning, and perseverance."

-Mia Hamm

☞**PRIMING THE PUMP:** Can you think of a time you won an award solely on luck? How did you feel about that? Has there ever been a time you didn't win something even though you worked harder than the person who won? How did you react to that? Luck happens. There is a saying, "The harder you work, the luckier you get." Explain what you think that saying means.

"I had no idea history was being made. I was tired of giving up."

-Rosa Parks

☞**PRIMING THE PUMP:** Think back to the day Rosa Parks refused to give up her seat on the bus. Do you think she was looking for glory and recognition or was she doing what she felt was the right thing to do? Explain your response. What serious risk was she taking when she refused to give up her seat? Can you think of a time you took a stand against something that you thought was unfair? How did you handle it?

"I hated every minute of training, but I said, 'Don't quit. Suffer now and live the rest of your life as a champion.'"

-Muhammad Ali

☞**PRIMING THE PUMP:** Ali usually fought two times a year during his great boxing career. How do you think he spent the other 363 days of the year? Do you think fights are won and lost in the ring or during the months of training? Explain you answer. No matter what your career or interests, do you think there will be days when you have to practically force yourself to get going? Did you know that Muhammad Ali is considered the most recognizable person in the world?

199

Perseverance QUOTES

"It isn't the mountains ahead to climb that wear you out; it's the pebble in your shoes."

-Muhammad Ali

☞**PRIMING THE PUMP:** On your way to achieving personal goals, you'll encounter many small, daily annoyances. What little things (pebbles) tend to aggravate you as you work on your goals? Can you always expect a smooth road, without pebbles? Sometimes pebbles can make us a stronger person. How can that be?

"Keep on going and the chances are that you will stumble on something, perhaps when you are least expecting it. I have never heard of anyone stumbling on something sitting down."

-Charles F. Kettering

☞**PRIMING THE PUMP:** If you haven't yet discovered your special gift or talent, how will you ever know if you don't take risks to try something new? Can you think of something that you attempted which you didn't think you'd like, but you did? Who are some famous people you've seen on television, or read about, that helped motivate you into trying new things?

"The vision of a champion is someone who is drenched in sweat at the point of exhaustion when no one else is watching."

-Anson Dorrance

☞**PRIMING THE PUMP:** Do you think a real champion is developed during all the regular hours of practice, or in those extra hours when the coach isn't watching? What are the chances of an athlete being truly successful if he or she doesn't give it 100% most of the time? When you are at practice and you see others cheating (e.g., not doing their exercises), how do you feel? What are some skills, gifts, talents you have which you often try to develop when others aren't looking?

Perseverance QUOTES

"The key is not the 'will to win.' Everybody has that. It is the will to prepare to win that is important."

-Bobby Knight

☞**PRIMING THE PUMP:** Do you agree with the part of the quote that says 'everybody has the will to win?' What are some of the reasons why people, who want to win, are not willing to prepare/practice to win? Can you think of a time you practiced hard, and your opponent didn't, and you lost? How did you feel? In the academic arena, have you ever studied many hours and got a low test score while one of your friends, who didn't study at all, got a higher score? How did you cope with that?

"People always told me that my natural ability and good eyesight were the reasons for my success as a hitter. They never talk about the practice, practice, practice."

-Ted Williams

☞**PRIMING THE PUMP:** Ted Williams, considered by many as the greatest hitter in major league baseball history, admits he was born with special gifts and abilities. But, explain why practice is needed to nurture those gifts. When you watch Tiger Woods drop a forty foot put, it looks so easy to him, but do you ever think about how many hours of practice he needed to develop his skill? What is a special gift or talent that you were born with, and how are you nurturing it?

"The amount that you are willing to sacrifice is directly proportional to your desire for success."

-Dan Gable

☞**PRIMING THE PUMP:** What are your thoughts when you hear a friend tell you how much they want something but aren't willing to pay the price (practice, sacrifices)? Let's say you want to be one of the best members of the Debate Club, what sacrifices might you need to make? If you really wanted to improve your GPA (grade point average) during your junior year of high school, think of a few of fun things you may have to give up for a while? Could you do it?

201

Perseverance QUOTES

"There are no secrets to success—don't waste your time looking for them. Success is the result of perfection, hard work, learning from failure, loyalty to those whom you work, and persistence."

-Colin Powell

☞**PRIMING THE PUMP:** Think of something for which you are successful. Then, if a younger person came and asked you for your secrets to success, how would you answer? Colin Powell mentions loyalty to those whom you work with. What is loyalty? How do you show loyalty to your parents, teachers, coaches, friends, and employer? On your way to success, how did failures and setbacks help you?

"Our society today has become so quick-fix oriented that nobody wants to work over a long period of time for one goal. They want it now!"

-Terry Stanley

☞**PRIMING THE PUMP:** Do you see some of your friends looking for shortcuts and quick-fixes on their way to meeting a goal? Why do you think people today search for the quick-fixes? Terry Stanley is a well-known marathoner. Do you think there is a shortcut to becoming a top-notch marathoner like him who can complete a 26.2 mile race in well under three hours? What happens to people who are always looking for quick-fixes and aren't willing to "pay the price" for success?

Perseverance

QUICK STARTERS

- *Shotgun Shuba's "600 Times a Day Plan"*
- *From Living in a Van to Living in Luxury*
- *Runyan, Legally Blind Runner, First American Woman Finisher in the 2002 New York City Marathon*
- *I Don't Want to Practice Piano!*

SHOTGUN SHUBA'S "600 TIMES A DAY PLAN"

George "Shotgun" Shuba was raised in a poor family in Youngstown, Ohio. He worked with his father in the steel mills. At the age of 16 he decided he didn't want make a life working in the dusty, dirty steel mills making low wages. He started to focus on his good baseball skills instead. In his book, *Positive Addiction*, Dr. William Glasser tells how George's hard work, determination, and perseverance helped him succeed.

George knew he was a good fielder; he could catch and throw, but he needed to improve his hitting if he was ever going to make it in the major leagues. He knotted a piece of string so a row of knots covered the strike zone from top to bottom. He hung the rope from a rafter in his basement. Then he took a heavily-weighted bat and every day from the age 16 through his minor league career he swung the weighted bat at the strike zone on the rope, six hundred times a day!

His hard work paid off. He got to play on the 1953 Brooklyn Dodgers championship team. Some of his teammates included Hall of Famers, Roy Campanella, Jackie Robinson, Pee Wee Reese, Gil Hodges and Duke Snider.

FROM LIVING IN A VAN
TO LIVING IN LUXURY

David Allen Sibley was always fascinated with birds. At the age of four or five he started drawing them and by the age of eight he was sketching them in the field. Throughout high school and early in college he explored many different careers but his true interest continued to be birds.

He took a huge risk, dropped out of college, bought an old van and headed out on the road. From 1985 to 1990 he traveled nomadically in a camper van searching for, and sketching, birds. He earned money by counting birds for agencies and leading bird-watching tours. For years he sketched and painted birds in excruciating detail, with every distinguishing mark on feathers, rumps and beaks. His collection covered 810 species of birds that live or pass through the United States.

After locating and painting the birds he began putting together a book. That took another ten or eleven years. The book, *The Sibley Guide to Birds*, contains more than 6,600 detailed illustrations and he designed it in such a way to make it user-friendly for the average person. The book, which was released in 2000, earned Sibley comparison's to two giants of bird illustrations: John James Audubon in the 19th century and Roger Tory Peterson in the 20th century. Since the release of this book, he has published several other books on birds.

Talk about perseverance! He pursued his interest in birds, quit college, lived in a van, located and painted 810 different species in six years, and then he took another 11 years to put the book together!

RUNYAN, LEGALLY BLIND RUNNER, FIRST AMERICAN WOMAN TO FINISH 2002 NEW YORK CITY MARATHON

In 2002, Marla Runyan was the first American woman over the finish line in the New York City Marathon. Her finishing time of 2 hours and 27 minutes was amazing! What also is amazing is that Runyan is legally-blind. She displayed the first symptoms of retina-damaging Stargardt's disease when she was eight. As her eyesight worsened, she became more determined to find something in which she could be successful. She recalls being very angry with doctors and other adults who discouraged her from taking on challenging tasks.

In high school she took an interest in distance running and competed, although without much success. She went to college, made the track team, but spent of the time on the bench. When she was 29 she got very serious with her running. At that time she had no coach and she suffered numerous injuries from falls. Her persistence paid off as she found good coaches who began to train her. Besides winning at New York, she competed on two Olympic teams.

A news reporter once asked her about her disability. Marla gave a powerful, thought-provoking response. She replied, "I think what I represent is achieving what you want in life. It's a matter of attitude. Some people have a negative attitude, and that's their disability."

Perseverance
QUICK STARTERS

I DON'T WANT TO PRACTICE PIANO!

When most people discover their special gifts and talents, they become self-disciplined and strive to nurture them. But that isn't always the case. Many actors, singers, athletes, and musicians share stories of their childhoods when their parents "forced" them to develop hidden talents. Now, these famous people look back to those days and thank their parents for being so firm, and consistent. Two such celebrities are Billy Joel and Jamie Foxx.

Rock & roller Billy Joel's nickname is The Piano Man. He is one of the most successful artists ever, selling millions and millions of CD's and albums. Every one of his concerts is a sell-out. But his piano-playing days didn't start out smoothly. His mother had to literally drag him, kicking and screaming to piano classes. He states, "I had to practice for an hour every day, weekends included. Before I could go out and play I had to practice. At age 11 or 12, I started getting cranky. I wanted to be hanging out with my buddies, so I stopped reading the music and started making up my own. The music teacher wanted me to learn Mozart. So she was very disappointed and said, "Your mother is wasting her money!" One interesting thing to add here is that Billy Joel made his daughter, Alexa learn to play piano. Now she has become a recording artist.

Actor, comedian, and recording artist Jamie Foxx had a similar start. When he was but a few months old his parents sent him to live with his grandmother. He thought she was mean because she forced him to practice the piano; he wanted to hang out with his buddies. Eventually he learned to like the piano, and his piano-playing actually helped him get the staring role in the movie Ray, which told the life story of the great Ray Charles.

Isn't it great that Billy and Jamie had adults in their lives that persevered!

Q
207

Responsibility

QUIPS

Responsibility QUIPS

■ Why be responsible?

Education, discipline expert Marvin Marshall reminds us of this simple fact:

Responsible people are happy people.
Happy people are responsible people.

■ It's always someone else's fault

Writer, Stanislaw Lee gives us this interesting quote to ponder; "No snowflake in an avalanche ever feels responsible."

■ I'm not responsible!

Explorer, Carveth Wells, traveled throughout the Malay Jungle in the early 1900's. The natives believed that cats were sacred and never should be killed. But, if cats misbehaved and killed chickens, they had to be let go. No one wanted to be responsible for the death of a cat, so they would tie the cat to a raft and float it down a river so that although it was successfully gotten rid of, no particular person could be accused of actually killing it!

■ The Four Rights for being responsible

If you aren't sure if you are being responsible, read the Four Rights.

Am I in the right place,
At the right time,
Doing the right thing,
With the right people?

■ Responsible robins

One of the characteristics of responsible people is their consistency. They almost always complete required tasks on time. How consistent are you? Can you compare your consistency to the American Robin? Check out this amazing example of consistency from Len Eiserer's book, *The American Robin*. At Williamstown, Massachusetts, for example, the average date of spring's first robin from 1816 to 1838 was March 15; a century later, during the years 1916 to 1938, the average was again March 15!

Q
209

Responsibility QUIPS

■ Are you a pursuer or creator?

There is an anonymous quote that reads, "Some pursue happiness, others create it." Which one are you?

■ Take responsibility for your mistakes

The famous football coach, Bear Bryant told his players that when they made a mistake, there were only three things they should ever do about it:

> 1) Admit it;
> 2) Learn from it;
> 3) Try not to repeat it.

■ Take a break!

It is very important to be responsible, but it always important to rest and relax on a regular bases to recharge your batteries. Author, John Lubbock, reminds us, "Rest is not idleness, and to lie sometimes on the grass on a summer day listening to the murmur of the water, or watching the clouds float across the sky, is hardly a waste of time."

■ A helping hand

The first person we should turn to when we need help is, ourself! Remember the Swedish proverb, "The best place to find a helping hand is at the end of your own arm."

Responsibility

QUOTES

Responsibility QUOTES

"Under normal periods, any man's success hinges about five percent on what others do for him and 95 percent on what he does for himself."

-James Worsham

☞**PRIMING THE PUMP:** Think about the percentages mentioned in the quote and give a few reasons why you agree or disagree. Can you think of situations in the classroom where students are too quick to ask for help rather than trying to work things out on their own? How is it possible that parents and teachers may actually be "hurting" kids by "helping" them too much?

"It may not be your fault for being down, but it's got to be your fault for not getting up."

-Steve Davis

☞**PRIMING THE PUMP:** What are some things that happen to young people that get them down, but are not their fault? How do you respond to friends who are always blaming others for their problems? What are some strategies you use to get "up" when others put you "down?" What options do young people have if they are living in a home where their parents are too strict, emotionally abusive, or physically abusive?

"The basics of a decent, civilized life are timeless; get up in the morning, take reasonable care of your body, mind, and soul; do some kind of work that benefits the world instead of harms it; respect and cherish other people; and then get some sleep."

-Bo Lozoff

☞**PRIMING THE PUMP:** Can you tell from this quote that Bo Lozoff believes that responsible people not only take care of themselves but, also help others? Explain why it is important to take care of our self first (e.g., sleep, exercise, etc) before being able to "truly" help others? What kind of work, activities, or volunteering do you do on a regular basis that benefit your community?

Responsibility QUOTES

"Do not worry; eat three square meals a day; say your prayers; be courteous to your creditors; keep your digestion good; exercise; go slow and easy. Maybe there are other things your special care requires to make you happy; but, my friend, these I reckon will give you a good lift."

-Abraham Lincoln

☞**PRIMING THE PUMP:** Lincoln gave this advice almost 150 years ago. Do you feel his advice is still relevant today? Explain your response. Looking at his list of recommendations, think of one or two you may need to improve on, and how you plan to do it. For the most part, who is responsible for making sure most of Lincoln's suggestions are met?

"I am not afraid of storms, for I am learning how to sail my ship."

-Louisa May Alcott

☞**PRIMING THE PUMP:** Explain how one's fears can decrease, the more responsible he or she becomes. What was a fear you had, but learned to deal with it on your own? How did you do it? Explain how a person's confidence can improve as he or she become more responsible.

"You cannot prevent the birds of sorrow from flying over your head, but you can prevent them from building nests in your hair."

-Malcolm Lowry

☞**PRIMING THE PUMP:** Is it possible to go through life and never experience sadness or sorrow? In the past year what was one thing that brought you sorrow and tell how you handled it. What are a few strategies you use to overcome sorrow? Explain why it could be dangerous thing to remain in a stage of sorrow for too long a period of time? Who do you turn to in times of sorrow?

Q 213

Responsibility QUOTES

"In our day, when a pitcher got into trouble in a game, instead of taking him out, our manager would leave him in and tell him to pitch his way out of trouble."

-Cy Young

☞**PRIMING THE PUMP:** Can you think of a time you got into trouble but your parents or teachers wouldn't help you? Were you angry? What finally happened? Were you able to resolve the issue on your and what life lessons did you learn? By not always helping you, are adults helping you grow as a person? What are some possible long-term negative consequences a teenager may suffer if he or she has parents that always "bail them out" when they get into trouble?

"There are plenty of recommendations on how to get out of trouble cheaply and fast. Most of them come down to this; deny your responsibility."

-Lyndon B. Johnson

☞**PRIMING THE PUMP:** Have you ever seen one of your classmates do something wrong and then deny it when confronted by the teacher? How did that affect you? Have you ever played on a team or worked on a project with someone who did not do his/her fair share, and, if you have, how did you deal with it? How do you feel being around others who seldom, if ever, take responsibility for their actions? Why do you think most adults want you to start your sentence with the word "I" when you fail to live up to your responsibilities?

"Keep away from people who try to belittle your ambitions. Small people do that, but the really great make you feel that you, too, can become great."

-Samuel Langhorne Clemens

☞**PRIMING THE PUMP:** As you strive to become a responsible young adult, others may try to belittle you. How do you cope with those hurtful individuals? Who is one of the most encouraging people in your life and how does he/she help make you feel great? What are a few things you say or do to help your friends feel good on their way to becoming successful?

Q 214

Responsibility QUOTES

"The U.S. Constitution doesn't guarantee happiness, only the pursuit of it. You have to catch up with it yourself."

-Benjamin Franklin

☞**PRIMING THE PUMP:** What does it mean to "pursue" happiness? Who is responsible for your happiness? What are a few activities you engage in that help you to be happy? How can the types of friends you keep determine the amount of happiness you'll experience?

Q

Responsibility
QUICK STARTERS

- *George Washington Carver Writes to a Student*
- *Responsible Behavior at Church*
- *Ben Franklin on Character Traits*

Q 216

Responsibility
QUICK STARTERS

GEORGE WASHINGTON CARVER WRITES TO A STUDENT*

George Washington Carver had become head of the agricultural department at Booker T. Washington's Tuskegee Institute in 1896. Following is a letter he wrote to his students in 1922. His letter offered them valuable suggestions for becoming responsible young citizens. Note: He refers to himself (the professor) as their father and he calls his students his children.

January 9, 1922

Mr. L. Robinson,
I wish to express through you to each member of the senior class my deep appreciation for the fountain pen you so kindly and thoughtfully gave me for Christmas.

This gift, like all others, is characterized by simplicity and thoughtfulness, which I hope each member will make the slogan of their lives.

As your father, it is needless for me to keep saying, I hope, except for emphasis, that each one of my children will rise to the full height of your possibilities, which means the possession of these eight cardinal virtues which constitutes a lady or gentleman.

1st.   Be clean both inside and outside.
2nd.   Who neither looks up to the rich or down to the poor.
3rd.   Who loses, if need be, without squealing.
4th.   Who wins without bragging.
5th.   Who is always considerate of women, children, and old people.
6th.   Who is too brave to lie.
7th.   Who is too generous to cheat.
8th.   Who takes his share of the world and lets other people have theirs.

May God help you carry out these eight cardinal virtues and peace and prosperity be yours through life.

Lovingly yours,
G.W. Carver

*This letter was adapted from the book, *Letters of the Century*, by Lisa Grunwald and Stephen Adler, Dial Press, New York, 1999.

217

RESPONSIBLE BEHAVIOR AT CHURCH

In his book, *Primer of Ethics*, Benjamin Comegys explained to young people in 1890 how they should behave in various settings such as school, home, in the street, and other settings. Following are his suggestions for responsible behavior in church. Enjoy reading these tips and compare them to how young people are encouraged to behave in church these days.

- Be in your seat before the services begin.

- Do not talk in church.

- Do not look at your watch during the service.

- Do not look around the congregation.

- Be quiet in church.

- Be ready to offer your seat and your book to a stranger.

- Do not use a fan to the annoyance of those around you.

- If you must fan yourself, do it very gently.

- Do not put on your gloves or overcoat until the services are all concluded.

- After the benediction, be perfectly still for at least a quarter of a minute.

BEN FRANKLIN ON CHARACTER TRAITS

Benjamin Franklin was known for stressing the importance of strong personal character traits. He also was known for setting weekly goals in order to improve his own traits. Here are the thirteen character traits that he stressed and a brief description of each.

Charity: Do you best to help others.

Cleanliness: Have a clean mind, body, and habits.

Fairness: Treat others the way you want to be treated.

Humility: Don't get a big ego.

Moderation: Avoid extremes.

Order: Don't agonize.......organize.

Pledge: Make a promise every morning to do your best today.

Productive: Work hard. Work smart. Have fun.

Self-control: Be determined and disciplined in all you do.

Silence: Be a good listener. Know when to talk and when to be quiet.

Sincerity: Be honest with your self and others.

Thrift: Monitor how you spend your money and your time.

Tranquility: Slow down and smell the roses.

Tolerance

QUIPS

Tolerance QUIPS

■ More oil please

Wilbert E. Scheer is credited with this very relevant saying, "Tolerance is the oil which takes the friction out of life."

■ Frown Power

Frown power originated in the 1940's as a way to discourage intolerance. This is how it works. The next time you hear someone make a racist comment, just look at them and frown. Your facial expressions may be more effective than words.

■ When the chess game is finished

Think about this clever Irish proverb for a few minutes. "After the game, the king and pawn go into the same box."

■ Are you helping?

Political activist, Jesse Jackson, encourages us to, "Never look down on anybody unless you're helping them up."

■ Taking a stand

By the 1840's many northern churches were taking a stand against slavery. Following is a bold statement from a pastor in Ohio to his congregation in 1845:

> *We regard slavery as it exists in our country a great sin against God and our fellow men…It deprives them of the unalienable right which God has given them of life, liberty, and the pursuit of happiness…And we resolve that…we cannot admit a slave holder to officiate in our pulpit or to participate in our communion.*
>
> -From the book, *A Stronger Kinship*, by Anna-Lisa Cox

■ Well, he looked like a thief!

Once upon a time a man whose axe was missing suspected his neighbor's son. The boy walked life a thief, looked like a thief. But the man found his axe while digging in the valley. And the next time he saw his neighbor's son, the boy walked, looked and spoke like any other boy.

-Lao-tzu

■ The Florida snow quieted the prisoners

David Wood, in the November, 2003, *The Sun* magazine tells an amazing story that happened one day in a Florida prison. It had been a normal day with much arguing, name-calling, and gang interactions among the men of different races. Then an extremely rare event happened. It started to snow. Many of the southern prisoners had never seen snow while men from the north missed seeing the white precipitation. Suddenly all the rudeness stopped and the men gathered together to watch it snow. A sense of calmness and peace hung over the prison.

■ It helps to know their customs

Whenever you visit other countries, it helps to study their customs. What you think is rude, may not be; it may be part of their culture. In the late 1890's, Colonel J.H. Patterson traveled to Africa to build new railroads. In one of his first visits with the Masai tribe, he was introduced to its leader. Patterson held out his hand in a friendly gesture, but the Masai ruler spit on him. No one told Patterson about the way the Masai greet visitors!

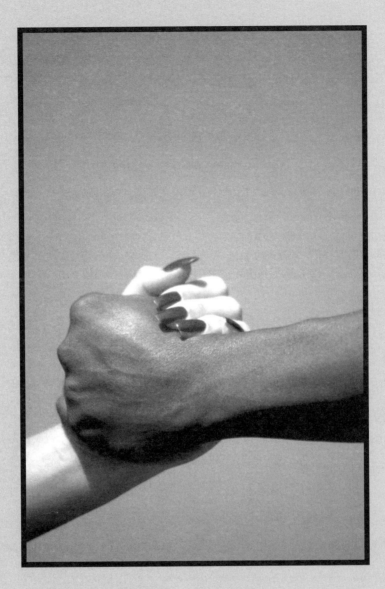

Tolerance

QUOTES

Tolerance QUOTES

"There is no such thing as an insignificant human being. To treat people that way is a kind of sin and there's no reason for it."

-Debbi Fields

☞**PRIMING THE PUMP:** Can you think of a time when someone belittled you and/or acted as if he thought he was "better than you?" How did you feel? Should both the janitor at the school, and the principal, be treated with respect? When you see students being rude and unkind to others, what do you normally do? Do you think it is important to go out of your way to be nice to those students who are teased or ignored? Explain your reasoning.

"I have decided to stick with love. Hate is too great a burden to bear."

-Martin Luther King, Jr.

☞**PRIMING THE PUMP:** Explain how hate can be a burden? Do you think it is possible to be a truly happy individual if you have hate for others? How do you think hate effects your health? Hate is a strong word. How do you react when you hear others use it?

"Those who hate you don't win unless you hate them back, and then you destroy yourself."

-Richard Nixon

☞**PRIMING THE PUMP:** When someone claims to hate you, how do you cope with it? What is the difference between "not liking someone" and "hating someone?" What do you think Richard Nixon means by "then you destroy yourself?"

Q

Tolerance
QUOTES

"World peace, like community peace, does not require that each man love his neighbor; it only requires that they live together with mutual tolerance, submitting their disputes to a just and peaceful settlement."

-John F. Kennedy

☞**PRIMING THE PUMP:** Is it possible that we could live in a world where we may not "love" all our neighbors, but we could tolerate each other? Explain your answer. How do you try to resolve conflicts with those you do not like? Can you think of a situation where you would seek help from a adult to help resolve a peer conflict? What is your opinion about the effectiveness of the United Nations in helping create world peace?

"Many people resented my impatience and honesty, but I never cared about acceptance as much as I cared about respect."

-Jackie Robinson

☞**PRIMING THE PUMP:** Jackie Robinson, the first black player in major league base-ball, mentions his desire for respect. What does the word respect mean to you? What are some things that others say or do that lets you know you are respected? There is a saying that notes, "Respect is earned." What does that mean? Think of one adult in your life for whom you have great respect, and, explain why?

"I have learned silence from the talkative, tolerance from the intolerant, and kindness from the unkind; yet strange, I am ungrateful to these teachers."

-Kahlil Gibran

☞**PRIMING THE PUMP:** Explain how one might learn tolerance from observing those who are intolerant? Can you think of a time when you saw someone who was so rude and unkind that it motivated you to be a kinder person? What did you see and how did you feel? Have you ever been around someone who was so talkative that it helped you realize the importance of be silent at times? How do you try to communicate with those who talk too much?

Tolerance
QUOTES

"All the races and tribes in the world are like the different colored flowers of one meadow. All are beautiful. As children of the Creator, they must all be respected."

-from the Native American
Indian Traditional Code of Ethics

☞**PRIMING THE PUMP:** How would you feel if you lived in a world with only one color of flowers? Explain how a meadow of different colored flowers is like a world with people with many different colors of skin. Should the color of a flower determine its importance? Are you aware of any book or documentation that proves that one color of skin is better than the others? What do you normally do when you hear people who claim their superiority based on their race?

"How far you go in life depends on your being tender with the young, compassionate with the aged, sympathetic with the striving and tolerant of the weak and strong, because someday in your life you will have been all these."

-George Washington Carver

☞**PRIMING THE PUMP:** What are some reasons we should be tolerant of the weak and aged? Almost everyone has an annoying habit. What are a few annoying habits that others have that you find difficult to tolerate? What is at least one annoying habit you have that others find hard to tolerate? What are some things that smaller children do or don't do that annoy you?

"None of us is responsible for the complexion of his skin. This fact of nature offers no clue to the character or quality of the person underneath."

-Marian Anderson

☞**PRIMING THE PUMP:** How do you feel about people who are quick to judge one's character solely based on skin color? Have you ever felt unfairly judged because of the complexion of your skin? How did you feel, and, did you do anything about it? Is it difficult for you to confront a friend who is too quick to judge another person? If you said "Yes," why do you find it hard to do?

Tolerance
QUOTES

"Prejudice is learned. Our children are not born with prejudices and stereotypes. It clearly is an attitude that is picked up. The key is to stop it as soon as it appears."
-Michele Borba

☞**PRIMING THE PUMP:** Do you agree that prejudice is learned? Explain your response. Where do you think most children pick up their prejudices? What are some things parents and teachers can do to encourage young people to be more tolerant of others? What role do the media (television, movies, music) play in influencing children's prejudices?

"We are a nation of many nationalities, many races, many religions—bound together by a single unity, the unity of freedom and equality. Whoever seeks to set one nationality against another, seeks to degrade all nationalities."
-Franklin Delano Roosevelt

☞**PRIMING THE PUMP:** The United States is known as the "melting pot" because we have so many different nationalities living here. What are some advantages of being exposed to many different nationalities on a daily basis? Think of a few foods you enjoy that are credited to other nationalities. How have immigrants added to the many different religious groups we have here in our country? Do you agree with Roosevelt that we should treat all nationalities equally? Explain your response.

Tolerance QUOTES

"Count no day lost in which you waited your turn, took only your share and sought advantage over no one."

-Robert Brault

☞**PRIMING THE PUMP:** How does "waiting your turn" relate to being tolerant? What are a few things that people take "more than their share" that display lack of respect or tolerance of others? What does it mean to be "used" or taken advantage of? Has it ever happened to you? How did it make you feel?

"The test of courage comes when we are in the minority. The test of tolerance comes when we are in the majority."

-Ralph Sockman

☞**PRIMING THE PUMP:** Can you think of a few times in your life when you were in the minority? How does that affect you? Think of two or three reasons why being in the minority can help build one's character. Think of a few ways you can build character when you are in the majority. What do you think Sockman means by "a test of courage?"

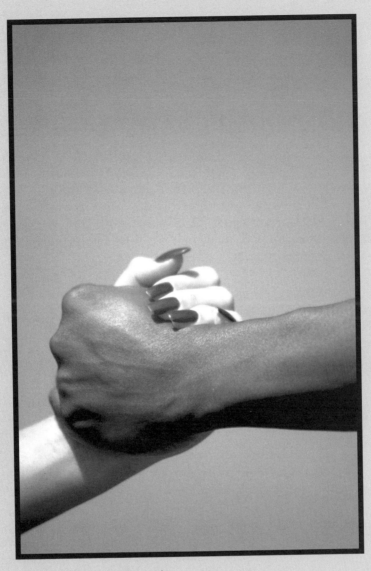

Tolerance
QUICK STARTERS

- Aaron's Brave Path to Success
- Four Faiths to the Rescue
- Booker T. Washington's Refusal to Hate Others

Q 229

AARON'S BRAVE PATH TO SUCCESS

For many years baseball fans regarded Babe Ruth as the greatest home run hitter ever. Few people believed anyone would hit more home runs than him; Babe hit 714. Ruth was everyone's baseball hero. Then, in the early 1970's, a young player named Hank Aaron started to get some attention as he closed in on Ruth's record. Ruth was white and Aaron was black. Many fans at that time couldn't accept the fact that Aaron might break Babe's all-time home run record. Aaron displayed an amazing amount of courage on his way to the record.

When Sandy Tolan was a sophomore in high school he wrote a letter to Hank Aaron encouraging him to press on to the record and telling him to ignore the racist people and threatening letters that were coming his way. To Tolan's surprise, Aaron wrote him back saying, "I want you to know how very much I appreciate the concern and best wishes of people like yourself. If you will excuse my sentimentality, your letter of support meant so much more to me than I can adequately express in words."

Many years later Sandy Tolan wrote a book about Aaron entitled, *Me and Hank.* The book highlights Aaron's frightening struggle to break the record. Here are a few examples from the book:

■ Aaron received thousands of threatening letters such as this one, "You are not going to break this record established by the great Babe Ruth if I can help it….my gun will be watching your every black move."

■ As he neared the record Aaron told his teammates, for their own safety, not to sit next to him in the dugout in case someone tried to shoot him. As a sign of support, his teammates continued to sit next to him.

■ During the chase to the record, Aaron had a 24-hour bodyguard. He stayed in a separate hotel f rom his teammates. Food had to be secretly brought to his room.

In April, 1974 Aaron broke the Babe's record. He ended his career with 755 homers. Hank Aaron needed great athletic skills to break the record, but more importantly it took a great amount of courage.

FOUR FAITHS TO THE RESCUE

One of the great things about living in this country is the willingness of people to help those in need. Many times people form somewhat exclusive groups based on race, nationality or religion, but they quickly leave their groups and/or beliefs temporarily behind when someone is in danger and needs to be rescued. The following story is a perfect example of people leaving their differences behind to help others.

During World II, the US ship, Dorchester, was torpedoed by a German U boat. There were four chaplains on board. Unlike most of the other sailors, the chaplains had gone to bed with their life jackets on. As the ship started to sink, many of the sailors couldn't locate their lifejackets. In an incredible act of selfishness, the four chaplains gave their own lifejackets to the other sailors, knowing that by doing so they would go down with the ship. Survivors noted that when they last saw the four chaplains they had their arms linked together and praying.

This act of courage was completed by four chaplains of four different faiths.
The four chaplains were:

    George L. Fox, Methodist minister
    Alexander D. Goode, Rabbi
    John P. Washington, Roman Catholic priest
    Clark V. Poling, Minister of the Dutch Reformed Church

BOOKER T. WASHINGTON'S
REFUSAL TO HATE OTHERS

One of Booker T. Washington's most well-known quotes reads, "I will permit no man to narrow and degrade my soul by making me hate him." This story is proof that he did his best to keep his word.

Booker T. Washington, the great black educator, founded the Tuskegee Institute in Alabama in the 1880's. I'm sure he taught many valuable lessons at his institute, but probably his most important was taught, not in a classroom, but while walking along a road. Although President Lincoln abolished slavery in the 1860's, many blacks were still being mistreated twenty years later. One day, Washington was passing a beautiful, large mansion owned by a wealthy white family. The mistress of the house saw him walking by. She did not know who he was and yelled to him, "Hey, you, chop me a pile of firewood right now!" He could have gotten angry and refused. Instead, he calmly took off his jacket and tie, and rolled up his sleeves. Several hours later he went to the front porch and told her he had finished. He handed her the axe and left. She didn't even say 'thank you.' As he was leaving, one of her servants said, "Ma'am, that man was Professor Washington!"

The next day, the embarrassed mistress went to Washington to apologize. He responded, "It's entirely all right, Madam. I like to work and I'm delighted to do favors for my friends." He created a new friend and, this new friend ended up donating thousands of dollars to his institute!

They Said It....

Following is a brief biography of all the men and women quoted in this book. A few individuals are not included because of a lack of valid information and/or identification.

Abdul-Jabbar: Former National Basketball Association player. He helped lead the Los Angeles Lakers to several championships. One of the all-time leaders in rebounds. Authored two books.

Adler, Mortimer: (1902-21101) American philosopher and author.

Ali, Muhammad: Former heavyweight boxing champion. Presently travels the world helping people overcome poverty, AIDS, and hunger. He is considered by many to be the most recognizable person in the world.

Alinsky, Saul: A criminologist who lived in Chicago in the 1930's. Known for his book, *Reveille for Radicals*.

Alcott, Louisa May: (1832-1888) American author. Her most recognized book is, *Little Women*.

Amos, Wally "Famous": African-American business leader. Rose from poverty to create his line of famous chocolate chip cookies.

Anderson, Marian: (1897-1993) African-American singer. She broke the color barrier by becoming the first Black to sing at the New York Metropolitan Opera. She had a United States commemorative stamp made in her honor.

Angelou, Maya: Author, poet, actress, college professor, civil rights leader. Her most recognized book is, *I Know Why the Caged Bird Sings*. Maya is a regular visitor on the Oprah Winfrey Show.

Armstrong, Lance: Seven time winner of the Tour de France, the most challenging bicycle race in the world. Twice recognized by *Sports Illustrated* as the "Athlete of the Year." Lance Armstrong, who nearly died from cancer, has helped raised millions of dollars to help find a cure for the disease.

Bartek, E. J.: Author, philosopher.

Baryshnikov, Mikhail: Russian dancer (ballet), choreographer, actor.

Baxter, J. Sidlow: (1903-1999) Australian pastor, theologian.

Bender, Sue: Author. Wrote, *Plain & Simple*.

Billings, Josh: (1818-1885) Humorist and lecturer.

Boom, Corrie Ten: (1892-1983) Christian Holocaust survivor who helped many Jews escape from the Nazis during World War II.

Borba, Michele: Author of the widely-used book, *Building Moral Intelligence: The Seven Essential Virtues that Teach Kids to Do the Right Thing*.

Brault, Robert: American poet.

Brezny, Bob: Author and writer of a weekly newspaper column on astrology.

Bronson, Po: Author of the popular book on careers, *What Should I Do With My Life?*

Brooks, Garth: One of the top recording artists of the 1980's and 1990's.

Brown, H. Jackson: Author of the New York Times #1 best selling book, *Life's Little Instruction Book*.

Bryant, Bear: Recognized as one of the greatest college football coaches ever. He coached many years at the University of Alabama.

Bushnell, Nolan: American electrical engineer and entrepreneur who founded Atari, Inc. and Chuck E. Cheese's Pizza Time Theaters. He was inducted into the Video Game Hall of Fame.

Burns, Carl: Author and English college professor.

Carlson, A. J.: (1875-1956) Swedish-American physiologist.

Carlyle, Thomas: (1795-1881) Scottish essayist, satirist, historian.

Carmichael, Chris: Lance Armstrong's coach and trainer.

Carnegie, Andrew: (1835-1919) Scottish born businessman and philanthropist. He was founder of Carnegie Steel Company.

Carter, Rubin "Hurricane": Popular boxer in the 1980's. He was accused of murder and spent many years in prison. Eventually he was found to be innocent and released. Now he spends his time trying to help other prisons who may have been wrongly accused.

Carver, George Washington: (1864-1943) African-American botanist who worked in agricultural extension at the Tuskegee Institute. He is widely credited for inventing numerous uses for the peanut.

Cerutty, Percy: Australian coach of many famous long distance runners and Olympian medal-winners.

Chao, Elaine: United States Secretary of Labor.

Chinmayananda, Swami: Hindu teacher who built many schools, hospitals, and nursing homes for the poor.

They Said It....

Churchill, Winston: He was the Prime Minister of England during World War II. In 1953 he won the Nobel Peace Prize in Literature. He was voted as the "Greatest Briton Ever."

Clarke, James Freeman: (1818-1888) American preacher and author who worked hard for the abolition of slavery.

Clemens, Samuel Langhorne: Known by his pen name, Mark Twain. This humorist and novelist wrote, *The Adventures of Huckleberry Finn.*

Coolidge, Calvin: The 30th president of the United States.

Comer, James: Professor of Child Psychiatry at Yale, author, and education expert.

Cryer, Gretchen: American playwright, actress, writer, and lyricist.

Cumberland, Richard: (1631-1718) English philosopher and Bishop of Peterborough in London.

Dalai Lama: Tibetan Buddhist peacemaker.

Dorrance, Anson: One of the most famous coaches ever in any sport. His University of North Carolina Lady Tarheels have won numerous NCAA championships in soccer.

Dreier, Thomas: author.

Einstein, Albert: German born physicist who formulated the theory of relativity. In 1921 he won the Nobel Peace Prize for Physics.

Eliot, George: English novelist during the Victoria era. She used a male pen name to ensure her words of wisdom were taken seriously. Her real name was Mary Anne Evans.

Ertz, Susan: (1894-1985) British fiction writer.

Feather, William: (1889-1981) American author, publisher.

Federman, Irwin: Chairman of the Board of the Sandisk Corporation.

Fields, Debbi: Founder of the Mrs. Fields cookie stores.

Florian, Douglas: Author of children's books.

Fonda, Jane: Actress, writer, political activist. She has won two Academy Awards.

Forbes, B. C.: (1880-1954) Financial journalist and author who founded *Forbes Magazine*.

Ford, Henry: (1863-1947) Founder of the Ford Motor Company and father of the modern assembly line used in mass production. He introduced the Model T automobile.

Frank, Anne: German born Jewish girl. She wrote *The Diary of Anne Frank* which details her story about hiding in Amsterdam with her family during the German occupation of the Netherlands in World War II.

Frankl, Victor: (1905-1997). An Austrian neurologist and psychiatrist. He authored *Man's Search for Meaning* which chronicles his experience as a concentration camp inmate.

Franklin, Benjamin: (1706-1790) He was one of the most well-known founding fathers of the United States. He was a printer, scientist, and inventor who invented the lightning rod. He published the famous *Poor Richard's Almanac*.

Fuller, Buckminster: (1895-1983) American visionary, designer, architect, author, and inventor.

Fuller, Thomas: (1608-1661) English churchman and historian.

Gable, Dan: Often called the 'Babe Ruth of Wrestling.' He won a gold medal in the 1972 Olympics and has been a very successful college coach.

Gaines, William: (1922-1992) Publisher of *EC Comics*. Best known for overseeing *MAD* magazine.

Gandhi, Indira: (1917-1994) Prime Minister of India from 1966-1977. She is considered one of India's most notable political leaders. She was not related to Mahatma Gandhi.

Garson, Greer: (1904-1996) Academy Award-winning actress.

Garagiola, Joe: Former major league baseball player and broadcaster.

Galbraith, John Kenneth: (1908-2006) Canadian-American economist who taught at Harvard.

Gibran, Kahlil: (1883-1931) Artist, poet, and writer who was born in Lebanon.

Glasgow, Arnold: World famous author and psychologist.

Glasser, William: American psychiatrist, education and behavior expert.

Graham, Billy: American Protestant Christian evangelist. A Gallup Poll placed him as #7 on the list of most admired people of the 20th century.

Grant, Curtis: Movie producer, actor. Helped produce the *Spider Man* movies.

Gurudeva: One of the great teachers of Hinduism.

Hamm, Mia: American soccer player. She helped the United States women win a gold medal in the 2004 Olympics.

Hanh, Thich Nhat: Vietnamese Zen Buddhist monk, teacher, author, peace activist.

Hayakawa, S. I.: (1906-1992) English professor and psychologist who served as United States Senator from California.

Henrichs, Garth: English author.

Hepburn, Katherine: (1907-2003) Four time Academy Award winner, star of film, stage, and television. She holds the record for most 'Best Actress' Oscar nominations.

Hirshfield, Tom: Well-known writer on the topic of creativity.

Hope, Bob: (1903-2003) British born, American entertainer. Performed shows for U.S. soldiers.

Horace: (65 BC-8 BC) A leading Roman lyric poet during the time of Augustus.

Howe, Edgar Watson: (1853-1937) American editor and author.

Hubbard, Elbert: (1856-1915) American philosopher and writer.

Hughes, Langston: (1902-1967) American poet, novelist, playwright, and newspaper columnist. Best known for his work during the Harlem Renaissance.

Inman, Raymond: A prominent figure in American real estate and auctions.

Jackson, Jesse: American politician, minister, and civil rights activist.
Jacques, Cheryl: Head of Washington-based Human Rights Campaign.

James, Henry: (1843-1916) American born author and literary critic. He was known for his novels and short stories on the themes of consciousness and morality.

Jefferson, Thomas: Third president of the United States.

Johnson, Kimberly: Author of children's books.

They Said It....

Johnson, Lyndon B.: 37th president of the United States.

Johnson, Magic: Former great professional basketball player. He now focuses much time and energy in the fight against AIDS.

Jones, Laurie Beth: Poet, author.

Jordan, Michael: Considered by many as one of the greatest basketball players ever. He helped the Chicago Bulls win six NBA titles.

Joyner-Kersee, Jackie: One of the all-time greatest Olympians ever. She won 5 medals in track and field events.

Kall, Bob: American author.

Kassinove, Howard: Professor at Hofstra University and one of the nation's leading experts on anger.

Keller, Helen: (1880-1968) Deaf-blind American author, activist, and lecturer.

Kennedy, John F.: 35th president of the United States.

Kettering, Charles: (1876-1958) Farmer, teacher, mechanic, engineer, scientist, social philosopher and inventor. He held more than 300 U.S. patents.

King, B. B.: One of the best and most respected 'blues' musicians in the world.

King, Martin Luther, Jr.: (1929-1968) American Baptist minister and political activist and the most famous leader of the Civil Rights Movement. He was a peacemaker who received a Noble Peace Prize. King is well-known for his speech, "I Have a Dream."

Kleiser, Greenville: (1868-1953) Author of the book, *Fifteen Thousand Useful Phrases*.

Knight, Bobby: One of college's most successful basketball coaches.

Latifah, Queen: Grammy winning American rapper, singer and Academy Award-nominated actress.

LaMance, Thomas: author

Lao-tzu: A major figure in Chinese philosophy whose existence is still debated. Lived in 6th century B.C.

Lee, Robert E.: (1807-1870) Celebrated U.S. Army officer. He was the general of the Confederate forces in the American Civil War.

Levine, Mel: Professor of Pediatrics at the University of North Carolina. He authored the highly aclaimed book, *A Mind at a Time.*

Lincoln, Abraham: The 16th president of the United States.

Lindbergh, Anne Morrow: (1906-2001) American aviator, author, wife of Charles Lindbergh.

Lowry, Malcolm: (1909-1957) English poet and novelist. Wrote, *Under the Volcano.*

Lozoff, Bo: North Carolina author. He leads a prison ministry and has won numerous humanitarian awards.

Lubbock, John: (1834-1913) English banker and politician.

Malloy, Merrit: One of the greatest poets of the 20th century.

Mann, Louis: American production set designer and art director.

Mantle, Mickey: Hall of Fame baseball player known for hitting many home runs for the New York Yankees. He won the Most Valuable Player Award three times.

Maugham, W. Somersett: (1874-1965) English playwright, novelist and short story writer.

Menninger, William: (1899-1966) Co-founder of the Menninger Foundation which is a well-known center for behavioral disorders. He also was very involved and supportive of the Boy Scouts of America,

Meyer, Joyce: Author, bible teacher, evangelist.

Mills, Billy: He was born in poverty on a Lakota reservation in South Dakota. He became interested in running and qualified for the Olympics and won a gold medal in the 10,000 meter run. His victory is still considered one of the greatest upset in Olympic history.

Moore, Joe: Humorist and newspaper columnist.

Muller, Wayne: Author and founder of the 'Bread for the Journey' which helps the hungry. He also works for a group that does research in the fight against AIDS.

Navratilova, Martina: Former #1 ranked women's tennis player in the world.

Nelson, Kevin: Long distance runner and author.

Newsome, Ernest: (1868-1959) English music critic.

Nietzsche, Friedrich: (1844-1900) German philosopher.

Nightingale, Florence: (1820-1910) A pioneer of modern nursing. She was also a noted statistician.

Nixon, Richard: The 37th president of the United States.

Noble, Charles C.: Author.

Obama, Barack: United States Senator from Illinois.

O'Connor, Sandra Day: First female Associate Justice of the U.S. Supreme Court.

Orben, Robert: American magician and professional comedy writer.

Osborn, Ronald E.: Teacher, researcher of church history.

Parks, Rosa: (1913-2005) African-American civil rights activist. The U.S. Congress called her, "The Mother of the Modern Day Civil Rights Movement." She refused to give up her seat on a bus to a white passenger in Montgomery, Alabama in 1955.

Pasteur, Louis: (1822-1895) French microbiologist and chemist. He is best known for demonstrating how to prevent milk and wine from going sour—pasteurization.

Payton, Walter: One of the best running backs in the history of the National Football League.

Peale, Norman Vincent: (1898-1993) Christian preacher and author. He is known for his book, *The Power of Positive Thinking*.

Picasso, Pablo: (1881-1973) Famous painter/sculptor. One of the most recognized figures in the 20th century in art. He produced over 13,500 paintings.

Powell, Colin: 65th U.S. Secretary of State and he became the highest ranking non-Caucasian government official in the history of the U.S.

Prather, Hugh: Minister, author, counselor.

Prefontaine, Steve: At one time he was the top-ranked runner in the United States. He died at a young age in a car accident.

Radmacher, Mary Anne: Artist, writer.

Renard, Jules: (1864-1910) French author.

Q 241

Retton, Mary Lou: American gymnast. She won 5 medals in the Olympics. *Sports Illustrated* once selected her as their "Sportswoman of the Year."

Rice, Condoleezza: U.S. Secretary of State.

Richo, David: Psychologist, author, and teacher.

Ritter, Josh: American folk singer.

Robinson, Jackie: The first African-American to play in baseball's major league.

Rochefaucauld: (1613-1680) French classical author.

Rogers, Will: (1879-1935) Comedian, humorist, social commentator, actor.

Roosevelt, Eleanor: (1884-1962) American political leader; wife of Franklin D. Roosevelt.

Roosevelt, Franklin D.: The 32nd president of the United States.

Roosevelt, Theodore: 26th president of the United States.

Rosen, Mark I.: Author, teacher, management consultant.

Rudolph, Wilma: (1940-1984). Born in poverty with 21 brothers and sisters, she survived polio to become the fastest women's runner in the world. She won 3 gold medals in the 1960 Olympics.

Sagan, Carl: (1934-1996) American astronomer and scientist.

Sayers, Dorothy: (1893-1957) British author.

Scheer, Wilbert: Author.

Schwarzenegger, Arnold: Actor and politician.

Seuss, Dr.: (1904-1991). Cartoonist and author of children's books.

Sheen, Fulton J.: (1895-1979) Television's first preacher.

Simon, Sid: Psychologist, author, college professor.

Sinise, Gary: American actor and Emmy winning film director.

Sivananda, Swami: (1887-1963) Hindu by birth, proponent of yoga, and author of over 300 books.

Smith, Sydney: (1771-1845) English writer and clergyman.

Sockman, Ralph: (1889-1970) American religious leader and orator.

Spelling, Aaron: (1923-2006) Film and television producer. He currently holds the record as the world's most prolific television producer.

Spurgeon, Charles H.: (1834-1892) British Baptist minister, known as the "Prince of Preachers."

Stallone, Sylvester: Actor who starred in the *Rocky* boxing movies.

Stanley, Terry: Long distance runner, marathoner.

Steinbeck, John: (1902-1968) One of the best known and widely read American writers of the 20th century. His most notable books include, *Of Mice and Men*, *Grapes of Wrath*.

Swope, Herbert: (1882-1958) American journalist.

Thomas, Isiah: Professional basketball player, coach, and team owner.

Thompson, George: Author and former police officer.

Thoreau, Henry David: (1817-1886) American author, naturalist. He wrote Walden.

Tolstoy, Leo: (1828-1910) Russian novelist. He wrote *War & Peace* and *Anna Karenina*.

Truman, Harry S.: The 33rd president of the United States.

Truth, Sojourner: Former slave who worked endlessly to help free other slaves after the Civil War. She also worked hard to allow women to vote.

Twain, Mark: See Samuel Langhorne Clemens.

Van Buren, Abigail: Known as "Dear Abby," the advice-giver.

Walton, Sam: (1918-1992) Founder of Wal-mart and Sam's Club.

Walton, William H.: A well-know figure in the real estate and investment community.

Washington, Booker T.: (1856-1915) Educator, author, and the first leader of the Tuskegee Institute.

Wayne, John: (1907-1979) Known as "The Duke." This Academy Award-winner is considered the top cowboy movie actor ever.

Weatherup, Craig: In 1988 he was appointed as president of the Pepsi-Cola Company.

Webb-Johnson, Cecil: English author.

White, E.B.: (1899-1985) American essayist and author who wrote the popular child's book, *Charlotte's Web*.

Wilde, Oscar: (1854-1900) Anglo-Irish playwright, novelist, poet.

Williams, Ted: Considered by many as the greatest hitter ever in baseball.

Wilson, McLandburgh: Author.

Wiman, Erastus: (1834-1904) Canadian journalist.

Winfrey, Oprah: Actress, author, magazine publisher, and host of her own television show.

Wooden, John: In his 40-year basketball coaching career his teams won more than 80 percent of their games. He led UCLA to ten NCAA national championships, including seven in a row.

Woods, Tiger: The top player and money-winner presently on the Pro Golfer's Tour.

Wright-Edelmen, Marian: Founder of the Children's Defense Fund.

Yeats, William Butler: (1865-1939) Irish poet won a Nobel Prize in literature.

Yogaswami, Sage: (1872-1964) Sri Lanka's most renowned contemporary spiritual master.

Young, Cy: (1867-1955) Hall of Fame great baseball pitcher.

Young, Neil: Contemporary folk, rock, and country singer.

Ziglar, Zig: One of today's most sought-after motivational speakers.